School Resources and Academic Standards in California: Lessons from the Schoolhouse

• • •

Heather Rose
Jon Sonstelie
Ray Reinhard

2006

Library of Congress Cataloging-in-Publication Data

Rose, Heather, 1971-

School resources and academic standards in California : lessons from the schoolhouse / Heather Rose, Jon Sonstelie, and Ray Reinhard.

p. cm.

Includes bibliographical references.

ISBN-13: 978-1-58213-121-4

ISBN-10: 1-58213-121-X

1. Public schools—California—Finance. 2. Education—California—Finance. 3. Education—Standards—California. 4. Academic achievement—California. I. Sonstelie, Jon, 1946- II. Reinhard, Ray M. III. Title.

LB2826.C2R573 2006

379.1'109794—dc22

2005036386

Foreword

Policy discussion of the state of K–12 education in California used to devolve into a discourse on the challenges of financing education, the effects of Propositions 13 and 98, and the power of teachers' unions. But beginning in 1995, a new element was introduced into the often-contentious debate—high academic standards, by which not only students but also teachers and the education system itself could be judged. It can be argued that the introduction of these high standards both reinvigorated the debate and increased the intensity of criticism by parents and the media.

The authors of *School Resources and Academic Standards in California: Lessons from the Schoolhouse* point out that these standards are among the highest in the nation—with test score goals equivalent to requiring that 70 percent of every California school's students achieve above the national median. To hold such high standards is indeed laudable. But how are they viewed at the local level, by those who teach students in individual districts and schools on a daily basis? The authors of this report—supported with funding from The William and Flora Hewlett Foundation—set out to answer that question at a select group of schools, interviewing district superintendents, conducting on-site school visits, surveying teachers, and conducting financial analyses. They found that the superintendents they interviewed were strongly supportive of the new standards regimen, chiefly because standards give them more direct authority over what actually goes on in their classrooms. However, the 2,000-plus teachers they surveyed were more ambivalent—supportive of standards but also concerned about the gap between the ideal of high state standards and the reality of low, present-day achievement levels at many schools.

Not surprisingly, neither superintendents nor teachers thought that the resources provided to school districts and classrooms were sufficient to achieve the high standards set by Sacramento. Teachers pointed specifically to staffing shortages, especially in areas such as student counseling and health services. And, following a growing national concern for more culture in the classroom, elementary school teachers in particular indicated their concern for what they viewed as inadequate staffing to teach art, music, and drama. The readiness of teachers to teach the content required by the standards was another worry, the authors found: Superintendents said that if given extra money and complete freedom to spend it, they would increase the number of hours their teachers spend in professional development.

One consequence of setting high standards for teacher and student performance is a more focused spotlight on the larger problems of school governance. At this point in the history of K–12 education, a great deal of the money and power rests in Sacramento. Court cases and popular initiatives have given the state almost complete control over the finances of public schools. The new, high academic standards are now also the exclusive domain of the state.

This centralization and standardization is occurring while teachers and superintendents struggle with the challenges of raising performance in low-income schools, which remain furthest from the 70th percentile goal. As long as Sacramento continues to call the shots on money and curriculum, individual teachers will be required to stick to the textbooks and teaching styles that will generate improved performance on standardized tests. But at the local level, flexibility, not just uniformity, is what superintendents and teachers need, to allocate resources within their district where they perceive the needs to be greatest.

This report suggests that a more equitable balance of power may well be required if these state standards are to be met and sustained and if individual low-income schools are to be given the attention they need to achieve those standards. With their more intimate knowledge of what it is like to try to implement standards in individual classrooms, superintendents, principals, and teachers may well have a better handle on how to spend the money than legislators in Sacramento.

David W. Lyon
President and CEO
Public Policy Institute of California

Summary

This report is the last in a three-part series examining the relationship between school resources and student achievement in California. The central focus in all three reports has been the standards-based reform of California public schools. Between 1995 and 1998, California introduced academic content standards specifying what students should learn in every grade. The question the state now faces is whether its schools have an adequate level of resources to meet these new expectations.

Our series of reports, funded by the William and Flora Hewlett Foundation, aims to help policymakers as they address this adequacy question. The first report, *High Expectations, Modest Means: The Challenge Facing California Public Schools,* provided an overview of resource adequacy by comparing California's expectations and resources to those of other states. That report documented that California has set some of the highest academic standards in the nation but lags in terms of resources. Our second report, *School Budgets and Student Achievement in California: The Principal's Perspective,* built on the work of the first by presenting principals' opinions about the resources schools need to meet the state's academic standards

The current report provides additional perspectives on the adequacy question based on site visits we conducted during the 2002–2003 school year at 49 schools in 22 districts throughout California. During these visits, we interviewed the principals and superintendents and we surveyed teachers. We also gathered financial data to trace revenues and expenditures down to the school level. The main purpose of this effort was to understand how California schools are responding to the state's academic standards, what resources they currently have, and what resources they think they need to meet those standards. Whereas our second report focused on the principal's perspective, this report provides results from interviews with superintendents, the survey of teachers, and the budget data.

The schools we visited were selected to provide a reasonable representation of the wide variety of California schools. Seventeen were elementary schools, 16 were middle schools, and 16 were high schools. They spanned the state's geography—six in Northern California, nine in the Bay Area, 12 in the Central Valley and Central Coast, 10 in the Los Angeles region, and 12 in the San Diego and Imperial County regions. Three-quarters of the schools we visited enrolled high shares of low-income students. The remainder served a more affluent student body. Although our schools represented a wide range of geographic and demographic characteristics of the state's schools, 49 schools is a small sample when considering the diversity of California's nearly 10,000 public schools.

Because of the limited number of site visits, generalizing the results to all California schools would be misleading. Nonetheless, much can be learned from actually visiting schools. Many of the people we interviewed had insightful observations about the resources schools have and need as they strive to meet the state's standards. This report should be viewed as a starting point for the discussion about school resources rather than as a scientific study of what schools have and need.

Local Responses to the Standards

The state has established an ambitious set of standards and holds schools accountable for teaching those standards. The state measures whether schools are achieving its goals through a battery of standardized tests given to students in each school. The student scores determine the school's Academic Performance Index (API), which ranges from 200 to 1,000. The goal for every school is an API of 800 or more and schools must make regular progress toward that goal, or they may face sanctions. Despite this formal state accountability system, the state must ultimately rely on districts and schools to carry out its vision.

The superintendents we interviewed seemed to welcome the state's vision. Although they pointed out several flaws in the reform's initial design, they endorsed the concept and seemed to believe that the state has steadily improved that design. In this sense, the standards were not an unwanted state intrusion in their districts' affairs. Rather, superintendents were eager to implement the state's vision.

Part of the reason that superintendents embraced the standards is that they give the district more authority over what transpires in the classroom. Because standards clearly define a teacher's job, they confer responsibility on administrators to ensure that teachers are doing this job. Thus, standards increase the authority of administrators and decrease the authority of teachers.

Some teachers naturally resent their loss of authority. In one district we visited, some teachers claimed the state standards violated their academic freedom. In most districts, however, teachers cooperated with superintendents and principals to implement the state's standards. Our survey revealed that teachers saw the standards as ambitious, as they certainly are, but few seemed to regard them as totally unreasonable. About 39 percent of teachers thought the standards were a realistic goal that could be achieved over time. Another 39 percent considered them a lofty goal that would be difficult to achieve. Only 12 percent described them as an overly ambitious goal that could never be achieved.

The superintendents shared a remarkably consistent view about the steps required to meet the state's goals: The first step required aligning the curriculum in their schools to the state standards. They approached this task by adopting appropriate textbooks and requiring that teachers work together to establish pacing calendars, which specify the lessons and standards to cover each week. The second step involved regularly assessing students to see which standards they understood and which they did not. The final step consisted of providing students who were struggling to meet the standards with additional support targeted to their particular needs.

Student Achievement and Family Income

One of the most challenging issues for standards-based reform is the strong link between student achievement and family income. This link is very clear when a school's API score is plotted against the percentage of students in those schools in the free or reduced-price lunch program, a typical indicator of low family income. As Figure S.1 shows, elementary schools with few students in the program typically meet or exceed the

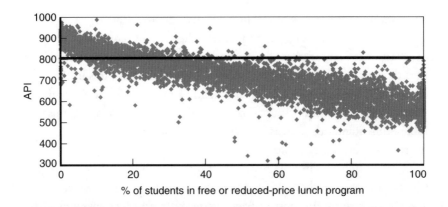

Figure S.1—Elementary Schools, 2001–2003 Average

state's expectations, whereas schools with many students in the program fail to meet the state's goal of an 800 API. A similar trend emerges at middle and high schools.

Because of the link between achievement and income, setting high standards for all schools inevitably focuses attention on schools serving many low-income students because they are less likely to attain those standards. Although what happens during the school day may partly explain the achievement gap between high- and low-income students, many factors associated with families are more likely to explain the gap. Low-income families cannot afford tutors when their children struggle with schoolwork and may not even be able to provide them a quiet place to study at home. Many low-income parents also have low education levels or may be recent immigrants with limited English-language skills. In these situations, parents may be poorly equipped to help their children with homework and may be less knowledgeable about the educational opportunities available. Because family income is related to these numerous other factors, we refer to it more broadly as socioeconomic status (SES) and often describe our schools based on whether they serve high-SES or low-SES students.

The teacher survey we conducted for this report reinforces the idea that low-SES schools may face greater obstacles to student learning than do high-SES schools. We asked teachers to rate the extent to which a variety of issues interfere with student achievement at their schools.

Teachers were asked to rate these issues on a scale ranging from 1 to 5, where 1 indicates no interference and 5 indicates a great deal of interference. Table S.1 lists the issues and shows the percentage of teachers answering 4 or 5, by the SES of their school. Between 56 and 68 percent of teachers in our sample believed that lack of student motivation, lack of parental support, inadequate English-language skills, and irregular student attendance posed serious problems for student achievement at their schools. These issues were much less prevalent in high-SES schools.

To the extent that schools can counterbalance the negative effects of low income and the factors associated with it, they may be successful in improving achievement among low-SES students by providing many of the extra resources that high-SES families can provide to their children. An effective after-school tutoring program could substitute for tutors that a more affluent family would provide. An extended school day or school year could provide students with a safe and quiet place to study with the additional support they need.

Table S.1

**Percentage of Teachers Rating Interference Level at 4 or 5,
by School Type**

Type of Interference	Low-SES	High-SES
Lack of student motivation	68	36
Lack of parental support	66	18
Lack of teacher training	10	4
Lack of school support programs	21	12
Too many students with inadequate English-language skills	56	13
Too many students with individual education plans	25	16
Student health problems	13	5
Irregular student attendance	59	22
Crime rate in school and surrounding areas	21	2

What Schools Have and Need

The strong link between student poverty and low academic achievement suggests that schools with many low-income students may need more resources to reach the state's academic performance goals. As we showed in *High Expectations, Modest Means*, districts with higher shares of low-income students do receive slightly more revenue per pupil because of various state and federal compensatory programs.

Using financial accounting data we gathered from 41 of the schools in our sample, we find that state and federal compensatory education funds are passed from the district to the school site where they were intended. On average, the low-SES elementary schools spent $431 per pupil more from these funds than their high-SES counterparts. Low-SES middle schools spent $368 per pupil more, and low-SES high schools spent $188 per pupil more than their high-SES counterparts.

Although this supplemental revenue did help contribute to higher total spending levels at low-SES schools, total spending differences are not as big as the compensatory funding differences would suggest. In elementary and middle schools, higher compensatory spending in low-SES schools was more than offset by lower levels of unrestricted funding. In part, low-SES schools spent fewer unrestricted funds because they spent less on teachers. In per-pupil terms, low-SES elementary schools spent $597 less, low-SES middle schools spent $207 less, and low-SES high schools spent $86 less. Differences in teacher spending can arise because either salaries or staffing ratios are different. For elementary schools, about 70 percent of the difference in teacher spending was due to differences in teacher salary, whereas 30 percent was due to lower teacher-pupil ratios at the low-SES schools. For middle schools, about half of the difference in teacher spending was due to differences in teacher salary and half to the teacher-pupil ratio. At high schools, all of the difference was due to differences in teacher salary.

One major reason for salary differences is the experience level of teachers. Although differences in experience may be important if they are related to student achievement, research has yet to establish a strong link between a teacher's experience and his or her ability to increase student test scores (see Rivkin, Hanushek, and Kain, 2005). We question whether differences in spending per pupil that result from differences in teacher experience represent true resource differences.

Given the small size of the sample of schools used in this analysis, it would be unreasonable to make too much of the particular results presented above. For example, geographic differences in wages and costs may also explain some of the spending patterns we observe. Nonetheless, the budget analysis provides the first step in understanding "what is." Only after we have answered this question can we ask "what should be."

The interviews with the superintendents and the survey of teachers help fill in the picture of what educators in California believe their schools need to be successful. We asked superintendents how they would allocate an additional $500 per pupil in permanent, unrestricted funds, and we asked teachers to identify areas in their school that were currently understaffed.

As *High Expectations, Modest Means* showed, California schools are understaffed relative to schools in other states. The teachers we surveyed during our site visits identified specific staffing areas they perceived as inadequate. About 40 percent of teachers indicated an inadequate level of staff for social and behavior counseling services as well as health services. Teachers also perceived the lack of technology support as a problem. However, these needs were reported consistently regardless of the SES of the school.

In contrast, most superintendents did not emphasize staffing when asked what they would do with additional funds. Their biggest concern was time for professional development, time for teachers and administrators to examine test results, and time to devise strategies for improving student learning.

Although most superintendents in our sample would prefer that state funds came with fewer restrictions on their use, most opposed completely unrestricted funds for two reasons. Restrictions were useful in keeping additional funds off the bargaining table and in resisting local political pressures to spread funds evenly across all schools rather than concentrating those funds in a few schools with higher needs.

School Accountability and School Finance

Standards-based reform has transformed the way public schools envision their mission. During our site visits, we saw this profound transformation firsthand. Standards have caused schools to focus on using their time more efficiently. They have also caused schools to identify students who are slipping through the cracks and to provide them with supplemental help. California's accountability system has also raised the question of whether the state provides schools with an adequate level of resources to meet the state's standards. Answering this question will inevitably raise difficult political dilemmas.

Establishing the same high performance standards for all schools naturally focuses the spotlight on those schools struggling to meet the goal. Generally, these struggling schools have many low-SES students and are likely contending with many complicated issues outside school that contribute to the achievement gap. Although it does not seem fair to hold schools accountable for factors outside their control, setting low expectations for children in these schools may become a self-fulfilling prophecy.

That achievement gap between low- and high-SES schools leads naturally to the question of whether additional investments in education should be targeted to schools with low-income students rather than spread across all schools equally. As our budget data show and as superintendents indicated to us, they find it politically difficult to allocate more revenue to schools within their districts with more low-income students. Given that difficulty at the local level, is it realistic for the state legislature to support such policies?

This question is particularly salient because, on average, schools in California have fewer resources than schools in other states. Parents in affluent California suburbs compare their schools with those in similar suburbs in other large states and quickly discover that their schools have larger classes, fewer counselors, and fewer resources overall. It seems difficult to believe that these parents will lend strong political support to investing additional public funds solely in schools in low-income neighborhoods when they perceive their own schools as inadequately funded. The logic of state standards may soon collide with the realities of pluralistic politics.

Contents

Figures

Tables

Acknowledgments

We are grateful to the superintendents, principals, teachers, business officers, and personnel directors at the 49 schools we visited during the course of this study. Our interviews and data-gathering efforts took substantial time from their busy schedules. We thank Gary Hart for introducing us to the superintendents.

We are indebted to Sharmaine Heng for her excellent research support and for keeping us very well organized through the hectic year of our site visits. For helpful comments on a previous draft of this report, we thank Christopher Jepsen, Paul Lewis, Marguerite Roza, Rick Simpson, and Merrill Vargo. We also thank the William and Flora Hewlett Foundation for their generous financial support. We appreciate the continuing interest of foundation President Paul Brest, Program Director Marshall Smith, and Program Officer Kristi Kimball in this topic.

Any opinions or interpretations expressed in this report are those of the authors and do not necessarily reflect the views of the Public Policy Institute of California.

1. Introduction

California is fundamentally reforming its public schools. The basis of that reform is a clear description of the academic content each school is expected to teach its students and a system of measuring whether students are learning that content. Ultimately, this reform may force changes in the way schools are financed and governed.

California's new academic content standards were introduced between 1995 and 1998. They describe what public school students should learn at each grade level in mathematics, language arts, science, and history–social science. The standards are detailed and rigorous; the Fordham Foundation rated them the best in the nation (Finn and Petrilli, 2000).

The state measures whether schools are teaching students that content using the Academic Performance Index (API). The API is the average on a battery of standardized tests administered to students in a school. The index ranges from 200 to 1,000, and the goal for every school is an API of 800 or more. In the first years of the API, the test administered to students was the Stanford 9 (SAT9). This test was first administered to a representative group of 450,000 students throughout the country, allowing a comparison between API scores and student achievement in the nation as a whole. If the distribution of student scores for a school mirrored the national distribution of scores, the school would have an API of 655 (Rose et al., 2003). As Rogosa (2000) showed, for a school to achieve an API of 800, about 70 percent of its students would have to score above the national median on the SAT9. In that sense, California expects its schools to perform considerably better than schools in the rest of the nation.

The SAT9 was not perfectly aligned to California's standards. To correct this deficiency, the state has added the California Standards Tests in English-language arts, mathematics, science, and history–social science. These four tests are not norm-referenced and were developed specifically to assess students' knowledge of the state's academic content standards. The state has continued to administer a norm-referenced test, however, replacing the SAT9 with another norm-referenced test, the California Achievement Test, 6th Edition. As these new tests have been introduced, the calibration of the API has been adjusted to yield consistency in API scores across time. As a consequence, an 800 API still represents a high level of performance.

A student's score on an achievement test reflects more than the effectiveness of the student's school. Other factors such as the education level of the student's parents may also play a role. To take account of such factors that are beyond a school's control, the state has created a Similar Schools Ranking, in which the API of a school is compared against the API scores of 100 other schools with students of similar backgrounds. A school with a rank of 10 would have an API in the top 10 percent of its 100 similar schools, a school with a rank of 9 would fall in the next 10 percent, and so on.

Although the similar schools ranking is a good way to judge a school's performance given the backgrounds of its students, the state expects all schools to achieve an 800 API, regardless of those backgrounds. Specifically, for schools with an API below 780, the state expects an improvement each year that is at least 5 percent of the difference between 800 and the school's current API. Schools between 780 and 800 are expected to increase their scores at a slower rate, but all schools are expected to reach 800 eventually.

California's explicit goals for its schools naturally raise the question of whether those schools have the resources adequate to achieve those goals. We have addressed that question in two previous reports. The first, *High Expectations, Modest Means: The Challenge Facing California Public Schools* (Rose et al., 2003), took a broad view of resource adequacy. It compared standards and resources in California schools with those in other states, traced the recent history of school finance in California, and examined the allocation of revenues across school districts in California. The second report, *School Budgets and Student Achievement in California: The Principal's Perspective* (Rose, Sonstelie, and Richardson, 2004), focused narrowly on resource adequacy. Using a series of budget simulations, it asked 45 principals from schools

2

throughout the state what resources a hypothetical school would need to meet the state's performance standards. Principals concluded that schools would need to increase their current funding level to meet the state's goals. However, principals disagreed about the specific bundles of resources schools need and about the achievement level schools could attain with a given budget level. This difference in opinion yields an important lesson: Although the adequacy question should be addressed, it is unlikely to have a definitive answer.

The current report presents a third perspective on that question. It reports what we learned from visits to 49 public schools located throughout California, where we interviewed principals and superintendents and took a survey of teachers. We also collected budget data for each school from its district's financial office. This report focuses on the interviews with superintendents, the survey of teachers, and the school budget data.

Although we attempted to select a representative group of schools to visit, it would be misleading to generalize the diversity of California's 9,000 schools based on visits to only 49 of them. But there is much to learn from actually visiting schools, including the reality of that diversity, which should be kept in mind as the state crafts public policy applying to all schools. We also learned that the people operating California schools have many perceptive observations about their schools—observations that can be helpful to policymakers. In short, this report is an exploratory, not a scientific, study of California schools.

The main focus of this exploration is how California schools are responding to the state's academic content standards. Chapter 2 describes the schools we visited, comparing them in statistical terms to all schools in the state. Chapter 3 reports on how teachers and superintendents view the new academic standards and what their schools are doing to meet those standards. Chapter 4 explores one of the most challenging issues for standards-based reform—the strong link between student achievement and family income. This link implies that although all schools are ultimately held to the same performance expectations, schools serving low-income students have more difficulty meeting these expectations. Chapter 5 examines the resources of the schools we visited, comparing the resources of schools serving low-income students to other schools. This examination leads to the issue of what schools need to be successful, which is the subject of Chapter 6. Chapter 7 concludes with some observations about designing a school finance system that directs resources to areas of greatest need. Because that design must accommodate the current system of governing California schools, the chapter also raises questions about that system.

2. Our Schools

In 2002, California had 9,087 public schools enrolling over six million students. Only 11 states had total populations that exceeded California's student population. During the 2002–2003 school year, we visited 49 of these schools in 22 school districts. We selected these schools to reflect the state's various geographic regions, student achievement levels, and socioeconomic status. Despite the breadth of the 49 schools we visited, the views we heard during our interviews do not necessarily represent those from all of California's diverse schools. Nonetheless, the opinions we heard during our visits provide a great deal of insight about what schools need to meet the standards. To better understand the perspectives of the superintendents, principals, and teachers in this report, and to get a sense of how applicable they are to the broader set of schools, it is important to understand the characteristics of the schools we visited.

This chapter describes how we picked the 49 schools we visited and provides an overview of these schools and their teachers. It compares our sample to the rest of the schools in the state in terms of location, size, student body composition, and academic achievement. We also describe the neighborhoods from which our schools draw their students. To provide this description, we linked data from the 2000 U.S. Census to the school attendance zone maps provided by the schools in our sample. Appendixes A and B provide more details about the data sources and how we selected the schools.

Overview of the Schools We Visited

We selected schools for this study to ensure that they represented key features of California schools. Specifically, we wanted them to represent all regions of the state and to include roughly equal numbers of elementary, middle, and high schools. Furthermore, we wanted them to represent schools from all parts of the distribution of student socioeconomic status (SES). Finally, as a practical matter of collecting budget data from district finance offices and the time involved traveling to school sites, we limited the number of districts from which we drew schools. Specifically, we ensured each trio of elementary, middle, and high schools we visited would be contained within one unified school district or a combination of an elementary and high school district. But within these criteria, we wanted the actual schools we visited to be randomly selected. To meet these goals, we designed a stratified random sampling procedure. To ensure that we had participants from each region in the state, we oversampled from smaller regions. Similarly, we wanted the proportion of schools we visited serving students from a low socioeconomic status to exceed the proportion of low-SES schools statewide. This condition was important, because low-SES schools are struggling the most to meet the state's academic standards and we wanted to ensure that we visited enough of those schools to focus on the strategies they had in place to meet the standards. Appendix B provides specific details about our sampling procedure.

We realized that not all schools would agree to participate in our study, so we selected more schools than we could visit—90 schools from 36 districts. To encourage districts and schools to participate in our study, we designed a multistep outreach plan. First, Gary Hart, former California state senator and Secretary of Education, wrote a letter to the superintendents of each district we selected introducing PPIC, describing the goals of our study, and encouraging superintendents to participate. Next, we contacted the superintendent of each district and set up a meeting. We visited those who agreed to meet and described the details of our study to them, often with the participation of principals of the selected schools within the district. Because we wanted the principals and superintendents to be candid during their subsequent interviews, we promised to keep the names of the schools and districts confidential.

Of the 36 districts we approached, 22 agreed to participate. These participating districts included 13 unified districts, four elementary school districts, and five high school districts. Almost every school selected from within those districts agreed to participate as well. Of the original 90 schools we selected, 49 agreed to participate. In two instances the superintendent felt that the schools we had selected would not be appropriate. In those cases, we randomly selected another school within the district with the same SES characteristics.

Our final selection of schools included about 60,000 of the state's six million students. Although our sampling procedure was based on a few simple criteria, we achieved a broad cross-section of schools. Table 2.1 compares the geographic distribution of the 49 schools in our sample to the statewide distribution. We visited six schools in Northern California counties and 12 schools in San Diego and Imperial Counties. Although nearly 40 percent of all schools and half of all students were enrolled in the Los Angeles region, we did not want the schools we visited to be dominated by this group. Therefore, we selected fewer schools from the Los Angeles region and more schools from the other regions. Because we undersampled from the Los Angeles area and because schools in that area had a lower response rate, we have a smaller share of schools from that region than is representative statewide. Oversampling, combined with high response rates in Northern California and the San Diego and Imperial regions, explains why our final sample has a larger share of schools from these regions than is typical statewide.

Table 2.2 shows more specific characteristics of the 49 schools we visited. Seventeen were elementary schools, 16 were middle schools, and 16 were high schools. Because we excluded small schools in our sampling procedure (see Appendix B), the schools we visited tended to be somewhat larger than the average size statewide. For example, the median elementary schools in our sample enrolled 687 or fewer students, about 100 more students than the statewide median. The median middle schools in our sample enrolled a few more than 1,000 students, compared to a statewide median of 915. Half the high schools enrolled at least 1,959 students, 242 students more than the statewide median.

The schools we visited were more impoverished and had lower test scores than is typical statewide, because we explicitly designed our sampling procedure to overrepresent that group. Half the elementary schools in our study had more than 76 percent of their students participating in the free or reduced-price lunch program. The statewide median was only 54 percent. As is typical statewide, a much smaller share of the high school students in our sample participated in this lunch

Table 2.1

Geographic Characteristics of Schools, 2002–2003

Region	Number of Schools Visited	Number of Schools Statewide[a]	% of Schools Visited	% of Schools Statewide
Northern California Butte, Colusa, Del Norte, Glenn, Humboldt, Lake, Lassen, Mendocino, Modoc, Nevada, Plumas, Shasta, Sierra, Siskiyou, Sutter, Tehama, Trinity, and Yuba Counties	6	535	12	7
Bay Area Alameda, Contra Costa, Marin, Napa, San Francisco, San Mateo, Santa Clara, Solano, and Sonoma Counties	9	1,467	18	19
Central Coast Monterey, San Benito, San Luis Obispo, Santa Barbara, Santa Cruz, and Ventura Counties	2	533	4	7
Central Valley Alpine, Amador, Calaveras, El Dorado, Fresno, Inyo, Kern, Kings, Madera, Mariposa, Merced, Mono, Placer, Sacramento, San Joaquin, Stanislaus, Tulare, Tuolumne, and Yolo Counties	10	1,617	20	21
Los Angeles region Los Angeles, Orange, Riverside, and San Bernardino Counties	10	2,906	20	38
San Diego/Imperial region Imperial and San Diego Counties	12	618	24	8
Total	49	7,676	100	100

[a]The number of statewide schools includes only elementary, middle, junior high, and high schools.

Table 2.2

Characteristics of Our 49 Schools, 2002–2003

Characteristic	Elem.	Middle	High
Number of schools			
Sample	17	16	16
Statewide			
	5,469	1,201	1,006
Median school enrollment (students)			
Sample	687	1,027	1,959
Statewide			
	557	915	1,717
Median % of students on subsidized lunch program			
Sample	76	68	39
Statewide			
	54	46	28
Median API			
Sample	717	635	625
Statewide	729	685	662

program. The median participation rate in our high school sample was 39 percent; the statewide median for high schools was 28 percent.

Given the strong correlation between poverty and test scores, it is not surprising that the sample schools also scored slightly lower on the state's API than schools statewide. Half the elementary schools in our study had an API of 717 or lower in 2002 compared to a statewide median of 729. The median middle school scored lower at 635; the statewide median was 685. For high schools, the sample median was 625, and the statewide median was 662.

Overall, however, the schools we visited performed slightly better than schools with a similar SES. Only 17 percent of our schools had a Similar Schools Ranking in the bottom 30 percent of similar schools. About 46 percent of our schools had a Similar Schools Ranking in the top 30 percent of schools.

In this report, we frequently group schools by the socioeconomic status of their students. The school's SES is defined by the percentage of its students participating in the free and reduced-price lunch program. This definition is somewhat different for each school level, because more students tend to participate in that program in elementary schools than do in high schools. Table 2.3 shows how the poverty and performance measures varied across schools within our sample, based on the SES category.

For elementary schools, low-SES schools had between 62 and 100 percent of their students on the subsidized lunch program, compared to a participation rate of only 2 to 30 percent at high-SES elementary schools. Statewide, 45 percent of elementary schools have more than 60 percent of students on this program and nearly one-third of schools have 30 percent or fewer participating students.

The low-SES middle schools we visited had 55 to 89 percent of students in the lunch program. Statewide, 40 percent of middle schools fall into this range. The high-SES middle schools averaged between 2 and 21 percent of students on this program. Statewide, nearly one-quarter of schools fall into this range. Our low-SES high schools had between 28 and 63 percent of students in the lunch program, but the high-SES high schools had 10 percent or fewer students in the program.

Table 2.3

Characteristics of Our 49 Schools, by Level and SES, 2002–2003

Characteristic	Low-SES	High-SES
Elementary schools		
Number we visited	11	6
Range of students with subsidized meals (%)	74–100	2–32
Average % with subsidized meals	87	13
Average API		
	683	843
Middle schools		
Number we visited	13	3
Range of students with subsidized meals (%)	60–90	1–25
Average % with subsidized meals	72	15
Average API		
	617	821
High schools		
Number we visited	13	3
Range of students with subsidized meals (%)	30–71	0–11
Average % with subsidized meals	44	5
Average API	616	796

About a third of high schools statewide fall into our low-SES range and about 22 percent fall into our high-SES range.

Not surprising, the high-SES schools we visited had substantially higher average API scores than the low-SES schools. The average API at the low-SES elementary schools was 683, yet the high-SES elementary schools surpassed 800. A similar trend holds at the middle and high schools—the low-SES schools averaged an API about 615, but the high-SES schools averaged APIs near or surpassing the state's goal.

To get a more detailed picture of the schools we visited, we collected maps of school attendance zones and linked them to data from the 2000 U.S. Census. Table 2.4 shows several census characteristics of the school attendance zones, revealing how dramatically different the high-SES schools are from the low-SES schools. The high-SES schools are located in less dense areas. On average, the high-SES attendance zones have 2,303 people per square mile, whereas the low-SES schools have more than twice that density. Median household income in the high-SES

Table 2.4

Average Census Characteristics of Our 49 School Attendance Zones

Characteristic	Low-SES	High-SES
Density (people per square mile)	5,677	2,264
Median household income ($)	39,054	75,208
Homes owned (%)	53	74
Percentage of population		
In same house in 1995	52	50
In same county in 1995	32	26
Married	53	53
With less than high school diploma	37	6
With high school diploma but no college	22	16
With some college but no bachelor's degree	27	35
With bachelor's degree or higher	14	43
White (non-Hispanic)	33	74
Black (non-Hispanic)	8	2
Hispanic	46	10
Asian (non-Hispanic)	9	10
Number of observations	37	12

areas is about $75,000—nearly twice that in the low-SES areas. Not surprisingly, more households in the high-SES areas own their homes—74 percent compared to 53 percent. Households in the high-SES areas tend to be slightly more mobile, in that fewer households were likely to be in the same county in 1995, but the differences are small. Marriage rates did not differ between the low- and high-SES areas.

Residents in the high-SES areas tended to be more educated; 43 percent had a bachelor's degree or higher and only 6 percent lacked a high school diploma. In the low-SES areas, the pattern is reversed; only 14 percent had a college degree and about 37 percent lacked a high school diploma. The racial and ethnic composition also varied substantially between these two types of areas. In the high-SES areas, nearly three-quarters of the population was white and 10 percent Hispanic; in the low-SES areas, 33 percent of the population was white and about half the population was Hispanic.

Overview of the Teachers We Surveyed

Forty-eight of the 49 schools in our study participated in our teacher survey. The one school that did not participate was a low-SES elementary school. The survey took about 20 minutes to complete, and we gave teachers a small honorarium for their participation. The survey instrument is available from the authors on request.

We had a very high response rate in our survey. Within the 48 participating schools, 2,764 teachers were asked to complete the survey. A total of 2,346 teachers complied, for an overall response rate of 85 percent. Table 2.5 shows how the response rates varied according the school level and the SES of the students in the school. Given the high response rate, the results we present in this chapter very accurately represent the teachers' opinions from our sample schools.

The teachers who participated in our survey had various levels of experience. As Table 2.6 shows, nearly 30 percent of teachers had four or fewer years of experience before the 2002–2003 school year. About half the teachers had 10 or more years of prior experience. The distribution of experience was fairly similar in elementary and middle schools, but high schools had relatively more teachers with 10 or more

Table 2.5

Teacher Survey Response Rates

	All	School Level			SES	
		Elem.	Middle	High	Low	High
Schools in survey	48	16	16	16	36	12
Teachers asked to participate	2,764	569	700	1,495	2,112	652
Teachers completing survey	2,346	529	591	1,226	1,749	597
Response rate (%)	85	93	84	82	83	92

Table 2.6

Total Years of Teacher Experience
(Percentage Distribution)

	All	School Level			SES	
		Elem.	Middle	High	Low	High
0–4 years	29	32	33	26	31	23
5–9 years	21	23	22	20	22	20
10 or more years	49	44	44	54	47	56

years of experience. Teachers in the low-SES schools we visited tended to be slightly less experienced than those in the high-SES schools. Whereas only 23 percent of teachers in the high-SES schools had fewer than five years of prior experience, 31 percent of teachers in low-SES schools were new to the profession.

Most teachers enter the teaching profession with a bachelor's degree and 30 additional units of university coursework that they accumulated during their credentialing program. As they continue in the profession, many teachers obtain a master's degree, in part to move up their district's salary schedule. Table 2.7 shows the education levels of the teachers in our sample. About 39 percent had a master's degree or higher. A little more than half had a bachelor's degree and 30 units of coursework but lacked a master's degree. The remaining 9 percent did not yet have the 30 units of additional credit beyond their bachelor's degree. Most often, these were teachers in a university or district internship program or

Table 2.7

Teacher Education Levels
(Percentage Distribution)

| | All | School Level | | | SES | |
		Elem.	Middle	High	Low	High
Master's degree or higher	39	31	32	45	37	44
Bachelor's degree + 30	52	59	59	46	54	48
Less than a bachelor's degree + 30	8	10	8	8	9	7

authorized to teach with an emergency permit. On average, high school teachers were more likely to have a master's degree. This result is not surprising given that high schools also had the most experienced teachers. Relatively more teachers in high-SES schools also had master's degrees, also an expected result given the higher level of teacher experience in those schools as well.

Conclusion

California is a diverse state with a diverse set of students. We visited 49 randomly selected schools that span California's geography and represent varying levels of SES and academic performance. Although 49 schools is a large sample relative to previous case studies, it is still a small sample when considering the vast array of California schools and student needs. Nonetheless, we selected our sample in a way that would allow us to focus on broad differences based on school level (elementary, middle, and high) and based on SES categories. The perspectives gained from the superintendents, principals, and teachers across these types of schools provide a solid foundation for an initial discussion about the resources schools have and need.

3. California's Academic Standards: A View from the Front Line

California's new academic standards are a clear call to change the status quo. The standards require that schools adhere to a common vision, implicitly overriding many local practices and preferences. The standards also direct California schools to aim high, to provide an education that is rigorous and comprehensive.

While aiming high is essential to improvement, aiming too high is empty talk. Goals that motivate positive action find the right balance between reaching high and overreaching. A test of that balance is how goals are perceived by those asked to pursue them. Do superintendents view the state's standards as another impediment they must overcome or a vision they embrace? Do teachers view the state standards as impossible or as worthy goals they and their students should strive to achieve? This chapter reports responses to these questions provided by superintendents and teachers in the districts and schools we visited.

Do Superintendents Embrace State Standards?

California's accountability system focuses on schools, not school districts. The state calculates an API for each school and uses that index to determine whether the school is meeting its targets for student achievement. The state's focus on the school as the unit to be held accountable inevitably shines the spotlight on the school's leader, its principal. Yet school principals are hired, promoted, and fired by school districts, not the state; and state funds for schools are channeled through these districts. School districts, in turn, are governed by school boards, elected by local voters who may not know or even care to know the state's educational goals for their children. There is thus a potential tension between a common set of standards for all California schools and the long-standing tradition of local governance of those schools.

This potential tension led us to wonder how school district leaders perceive the state's new emphasis on standards and accountability. Are district leaders willing to act as agents for the state as implicitly demanded by the new accountability system, or do they perceive the state standards as limiting their own authority? Do district leaders see the state standards as contravening the dictates of the elected representatives to whom they are ultimately responsible? To address these questions, we interviewed the superintendents of the schools we visited.

Despite their general reservations about any requirements the state imposes on their districts, the superintendents we interviewed strongly supported the concept of state standards and accountability. Although some had criticisms of the way that system has been implemented, even those critics emphasized that they supported the general concept. None complained that state standards had eroded their authority. In fact, most seemed to welcome rigorous standards because such standards increased their authority over what was transpiring in the classroom.

One superintendent in an affluent, suburban district put it this way:

> When I was a teacher, it wasn't really clear to me what I was expected to attain with my students. Now, at least for teachers in this district, that is very clear.

A superintendent in a small, rural elementary district stated it more directly. Her message to teachers was this:

> Do not teach a lesson unless there's a standard attached to it. Now when you teach all the standards and the kids know all those standards, then you can have your little cutesy lessons. Sorry, but our teachers were teaching what they wanted, and with anything they wanted.

This superintendent's only regret was that standards hadn't been introduced 20 years previously.

In addition to controlling classroom curriculum, several superintendents contended that standards had helped clarify what parents and students should expect from their schools. One superintendent of a middle-class suburban district said,

> Standards made us, as a profession, step up to the plate, analyze what we're doing, and share that information with our customers, which is very, very different than before standards.

This district had created standards-based report cards for its elementary students and engaged in an extensive public relations campaign to explain the report card and the state standards to parents. In a district survey of parents, more than 90 percent responded that they were familiar with the standards for their children's grade levels. Several elementary schools in other districts had standards-based report cards for students, including one large urban district that had also undertaken an extensive effort to educate parents about what their children were expected to learn in each grade. These districts have used academic standards to clarify for parents the education their children should receive, making it easier for parents to become active agents in ensuring that their children receive that education.

If state standards have increased management authority over teachers, it is teachers, not district leaders, who have lost authority in this process. In the words of one experienced superintendent in a small city in the Central Valley,

> The world of instruction has traditionally been behind that closed door. It is no longer behind that closed door, and that has given principals incredible leverage. The state has said, "Thou shalt do this." Now, it's *how* we need to get it done, not *if* we need to get it done. I'm sure there are teachers in every school who resent the heck out of that.

In fact, in one middle-class suburban district we visited, the teachers' union maintained that the state's standards violated its teachers' right to academic freedom. As described by its superintendent,

> Principals had the standards on their shelves and available to teachers. But because of the contract they were not allowed to give the standards out to teachers. Because of academic freedom, teachers believe that they can teach what they want, when they want, how they want, without regards to what students need. It all goes back to academic freedom. If they don't want to assess, it's academic freedom. If they don't want to teach the standards, you can't tell them to teach the standards.

It is worth noting that the elementary school we visited in that district did follow the standards very closely. It had established pacing calendars tied to state standards, and its students did quite well on the state's annual tests. A former principal at that school explained to us that the teachers in the school had voluntarily agreed to follow the state's standards. The standards did not violate their academic freedom because they were not imposed on them, in their view. In other schools in the district, teachers had not made that choice.

Other superintendents reported that their teachers' union initially had reservations about state standards, but those reservations had been overcome. A superintendent of a rural district in Northern California described the initial reservations this way:

> The union came to me and told me, "We decide what's taught." And I said, "No, you don't. The district decides what's taught, and you have the ability to determine how to teach it. But you're responsible to make sure it's learned, not just taught, but learned."

After this initial confrontation, the teachers began to take a more positive view toward standards and to have real success. In fact, the elementary school we visited in this district had met its API growth targets for several successive years. The superintendent believed that the change in teachers' attitudes was due to the positive effect standards had on less effective teachers. In her words,

> The thing that the teachers liked was the accountability. Because they watched teachers not doing their jobs, and they were ticked off at them. And so they decided that accountability was a good thing, because we were going to make the bad teachers do their job.

In another large suburban district we visited, the superintendent was careful to point out that the teachers' union in his district strongly supported state standards. He referred specifically to the district's peer assistance and review board, which can recommend remedial actions, including dismissal, for teachers with sub-par performance. The board is composed of both district and union representatives, and the superintendent claimed that we would be hard pressed to distinguish the union representatives from the management representatives.

It is understandable that some teachers regard state standards as an unwelcome intrusion, but it is also important to remember that teachers are relatively insulated from external pressures. Principals do evaluate their teachers regularly; but once a teacher has permanent status, it is very difficult to remove him or her. Furthermore, those evaluations do not affect a teacher's salary, which is solely determined by the teacher's education and years of experience. Although state standards are focused on the classroom, the teachers in those classrooms face few consequences if their students fail to demonstrate proficiency on state tests.

Not so for principals. Standards and accountability have increased the leverage of principals, but they have also increased the pressure on them to reach performance goals. The API is a measure of a school's performance, which reflects on its principal. One superintendent in a large urban district described the housecleaning during his first few years on the job:

> We fired every principal who couldn't do it. I had principals call me up after they got their test scores and ask, "Am I fired?"

In another large urban district, one principal we visited told us that she expected to be removed because test scores at her school had not risen during her tenure. As predicted, she was gone by the end of the year. The survivors of this winnowing process have reason to be proud. The superintendent quoted immediately above also told us what he said to principals at a districtwide meeting:

> If you're not good, you're not going to be here. I want you to look around and say, these are great people. And people came up to me after and said, "That's a tough message, but, by God, it feels good."

We heard this tough message in other school districts. Under the state's new accountability system, principals have more visibility, leverage, and pressure. These new conditions may attract a different type of person to the job of principal, a person who is drawn to a well-defined challenge and can handle the pressure that comes with it. However, it must also be a person who can work cooperatively with teachers, because, in a real sense, principals do not have any more authority over teachers than they had before.

Despite their overwhelming support for the concept of standards and accountability, superintendents had several reservations about the implementation of standards. Several expressed the concern that the SAT9, the first standardized test required by the state under the new system, was not aligned to the standard. As one superintendent put it,

Only now that we've moved into a more authentic kind of assessment, where we're tying what we're teaching in the state to the assessment, are we starting to get some measure of actually what we're doing in schools. The way that it was being done and what they were looking for seemed to be at odds, but we're kind of coming into line.

Several superintendents also expressed concern over the on-again, off-again nature of the high school exit exam. The exam was first targeted for the high school class of 2004. Ninth graders in this class were given the opportunity to take the exam for the first time in the spring of 2001. The following spring, tenth graders who had not passed the test were required to take the exam. However, in July 2003, the State Board of Education postponed full implementation of the exit exam until the class of 2006. Although the classes of 2003 and 2004 were required to take the exam, they were not required to pass it to receive a high school diploma. Postponing the exam undercut some school districts that had been alerting their students and communities about the new requirement for high school graduation. One superintendent in a Central Valley city had worked diligently to prepare his community for the high school exit exam and the virtual certainty that some students would fail that exam despite completing four years of high school. This district had created an alternative certificate of attendance for such students and had gone to great lengths to explain to potential employers that a high school diploma was a measure of academic achievement and not necessarily a measure of a person's value in the workplace. In this blue collar community with many low skill jobs, some employers may value diligence and reliability more than the knowledge of algebra. At the same time, the district had emphasized the importance of the high school exit exam to its students and had set up special tutoring sessions for students in the class of 2004 who had not yet passed the exam. The superintendent was understandably discouraged by the postponement of the exit exam, which was his primary motivation for this statement:

I'm very positive about state testing and accountability. I haven't been as excited about the implementation. It's been very jerky and less than efficiently implemented. Every time we get really going, things change on us, so the jerkiness of the implementation has been the only downside.

Another concern expressed by superintendents was that the state standards were too broad, particularly in the sciences and social sciences. Even in the most affluent district we visited, a district in which almost all students are expected to go on to college and most do, the superintendent believed that the State Board of Education had failed to make the difficult choices that would distinguish essential knowledge from a list of laudable aspirations. In his words,

> You can't do it all, and that's the fundamental problem with the state standards. It's too bad, because we had an extraordinary opportunity to do it right. It's going to take some serious political change now in order to revise those standards so that there's more depth and less breadth.

Most districts we visited have addressed this perceived overreach by adopting "power" or "essential" standards, a subset of state standards that the district believes to be particularly important. In forming this subset, many districts have looked to the frequency with which standards are tested on state exams. In that sense, the exams have played the role of an informal revision and tightening of the state standards.

Despite these difficulties superintendents identified, we came away from our visits with the strong impression that they strongly supported the general philosophy behind the state's new system of standards and accountability. In fact, their biggest general concern was whether the state would follow through on the reforms it had initiated. Most superintendents believed that their districts were making positive changes in response to the state's standards, but they also saw much more to accomplish. These accomplishments would be more likely if the state were to steer a steady course.

How Do Teachers View the New Standards?

Teachers bring a different perspective to this reform. Superintendents may have a broad perspective, but teachers confront the daily challenges of educating their students according to the state's new vision. If the standards are too broad, teachers will find it impossible to turn those standards into a viable curriculum. If the State Board aims too high, even the best teachers will fail to meet its expectations. Accordingly, we asked teachers in the schools we visited whether California's standards were (1) an overly ambitious goal that can never be achieved, (2) a lofty goal that will be difficult to achieve, or (3) a realistic goal that can be achieved over time. Table 3.1 summarizes their responses.

Those responses differed by school level. Elementary school teachers were less likely than middle and high school teachers to respond that standards were impossible to achieve and more likely to respond that the standards were realistic. This pattern is understandable because in the early grades, the standards focus on language and mathematics. As students progress, the standards widen and become less focused. A good example is the history standard for sixth graders, which one principal referred to as the "five by six" standard. Students are to analyze the five elements—geographic, political, economic, religious, and social structures—of six ancient civilizations—Mesopotamia, the Ancient Hebrews, Ancient Greece, India, China, and Rome. In the seventh grade, they analyze the same five elements of six civilizations during the Middle Ages. Nothing in the elementary curriculum is quite as extensive.

The sixth and seventh grade history standards are not anomalies. In twelfth grade, economics is half of a social science standard labeled "Principles of American Democracy and Economics." The material described in that standard would be comparable to that presented in a year-long course in economic principles at the University of California.[1] There are similar examples in the science standards.

Table 3.1

Teachers' Characterization of Academic Standards, by School Level
(Percentage Distribution)

Characterization	All	Elem.	Middle	High
Overly ambitious goal that can never be achieved	12	6	14	14
Lofty goal that will be very difficult to achieve	39	44	38	38
Realistic goal that can be achieved over time	39	46	39	37
Do not know, have not seen standards	1	0	1	1
Does not apply/missing	8	3	9	10

---

[1] One of the authors of this report teaches the introductory course in economic principles at the University of California, Santa Barbara.

If the science, history, and social science standards are too broad in the upper grades, teachers of those subjects would be more likely to respond that the standards are unrealistic. In fact, that appears to be true. Table 3.2 gives responses of middle and high school teachers by their academic specializations. Forty percent of English teachers view the standards as a realistic goal. This percentage is not as high as that of elementary school teachers, but it is five points higher than the percentages of history and science teachers who hold the same view of their standards. The percentage for English teachers is also higher than for math teachers. In the case of mathematics, the standards are not necessarily too broad as they may be in history and science, but they are very ambitious. Every student is expected to learn algebra by the eighth grade, a requirement many schools we visited were struggling to meet. Experience may also affect a teacher's view of California's standards. More experienced teachers may have a better sense of what students can reasonably achieve. They may also be more set in their ways and more likely to view the standards as a challenge to those practices. On the other hand, new teachers are more likely to have been exposed to standards-based education in their training and thus more likely to believe in its effectiveness. In any event, experienced teachers were less likely to respond that the standards are realistic and more likely to conclude that they are overly ambitious (Table 3.3). Overall, however, experienced teachers were not much different from inexperienced teachers in their opinions about California's standards.

Table 3.2

Teachers' Characterization of Academic Standards, by Academic Specialization (Percentage Distribution)

Characterization	English	History/ Social Science	Math	Science
Overly ambitious goal that can never be achieved	16	19	17	11
Lofty goal that will be very difficult to achieve	42	41	44	49
Realistic goal that can be achieved over time	40	35	36	35
Do not know, have not seen standards	0	0	1	0
Does not apply/missing	2	4	2	5

Table 3.3

Teachers' Characterization of Academic Standards, by Years of Experience (Percentage Distribution)

Characterization	0–4 Years	5–9 Years	10+ Years
Overly ambitious goal that can never be achieved	10	12	13
Lofty goal that will be very difficult to achieve	39	39	40
Realistic goal that can be achieved over time	42	40	37
Do not know, have not seen standards	1	1	1
Does not apply/missing	7	8	9

The most surprising result of our survey is the high percentage of teachers who view the standards as a realistic goal—about 40 percent. In contrast, only 12 percent of teachers responded that the goals could never be achieved. This generally optimistic response may in part reflect what schools and districts have done to narrow the state's standards to a more manageable set of essential standards. Whatever the reason, it seems to us that the responses overall suggest that teachers believe that the State Board of Education got the standards about right. At the least, the teachers we surveyed have not dismissed the new standards out of hand.

Teachers had many reservations about the state-mandated tests, however, which they registered in written answers to open-ended questions in our survey. Many complained about the time schools devoted to those tests. One teacher wrote,

> The state testing program is the single most destructive influence in schools today. We waste more time worrying about the results than they warrant.

Another raised a concern that will resonate with any experienced teacher:

> Never give students a test that they have no motive to do well on!

In response to this concern, several schools had taken concrete steps to encourage students to do well on state tests, including material rewards and appeals to school pride.

We expected teachers to criticize state-mandated tests, and we understood much of that criticism. In fact, however, the criticism was less widespread than we expected. Teachers raised legitimate concerns, but they also wrote about many of the positive actions their schools were taking to increase student achievement on those tests. Their open-ended responses to our survey showed that most teachers in the schools we visited seemed generally to accept the state's academic standards and its method of measuring whether students had achieved those standards.

How Are Districts Responding to the New Standards?

The districts we visited are in various stages in responding to the new era of state standards. Despite these differences, we perceived a common, general approach, which can be broken down into three phases. Phase one is aligning school curriculum to cover essential state standards, phase two is developing assessment tools to determine whether students are mastering those standards, and phase three is implementing targeted interventions to help students who are failing to learn required material through the regular course of instruction. We would describe the underlying model behind this approach in the following oversimplified way: a regular classroom program that moves as many students as possible to proficiency, backed up by a series of targeted interventions for students who fail to achieve proficiency. As we explained in Rose, Sonstelie, and Richardson (2004), this model seemed to inform the thinking of many of the principals in our budget simulations. In allocating their budgets, they struggled to balance the goal of having small classes in their regular program against the goal of having a well-staffed tutoring program.

An important element of the first phase is adopting textbooks that are aligned to state standards. At the time we visited, many districts were only partially through this process. As superintendents emphasized, however, essential standards and textbooks aligned to standards are not by themselves enough to guarantee that the state-mandated curriculum is adequately covered. A superintendent in one large suburban district told us,

> To give a teacher a new book and believe that they will have a sense of how to get through this material, we have learned is not realistic.

In addition to new textbooks, teachers also need pacing calendars describing where they should be during each week in the school year.

Ideally, these calendars describe chapters of the textbook to be covered and the standards to be emphasized each week. Typically, these calendars are worked out by teams of teachers, as they work through the material and consult with each other. The calendars are also revised year to year as teachers gain more experience with the material. In general, the pacing calendars are a collaborative effort to ensure that every teacher devotes sufficient time to each important topic but also moves through the material quickly enough to cover all the required topics during the school year. Implicit in these calendars are effective teaching strategies that engage students and teach them the lessons they need to master. In our observations, these calendars and the strategies underlying them were constantly evolving as teachers learned from their experiences.

The second phase is ongoing assessment to determine what students are learning as they progress through the year. Most of the districts we visited pay close attention to student performance on the state-mandated tests at the end of the year, and those results may be useful in identifying systematic weaknesses in the instructional program. However, because the results are not reported for several more months, they are not that useful in diagnosing difficulties that individual students are having during the year. In several districts we visited, superintendents stressed the importance of doing a better job with ongoing individual assessment. One superintendent in a Central Valley high school district described this need:

> The data analysis is at a certain level in our district, and we're doing a
> reasonably good job of it, but it's got to be more intense, digging down into
> the minutia of the data and saying, these are where the weaknesses are, not
> only in groups of kids but in individuals.

This district had created its own system of tests by subject area and administers those tests to students every six weeks during the year. Teachers in the district's schools also had the results of these assessments and the state tests displayed on their computers for each student in every class. The challenge facing the district now was a good analysis of those test results. In a similar vein, a superintendent of a large, suburban district said,

> The single biggest thing that we have to do is make sure that for every one of
> our kids we've done a good diagnosis, a good prescription, and follow through

on them. Rather than saying, gee, they all can't read, we're going to have them do phonics, you look at the groups of kids and what their needs are, whether it's a particular after-school program or a class.

The elementary school that we visited in this district used a software program named AssessmentMaster, which was developed by Renaissance Learning. The program allowed schools to easily develop a student test tied to California's standards. The completed tests could then be scanned and sent to a central facility for analysis. The analysis indicated which standards individual students or entire classrooms needed more time with to master. Our sense was that most districts we visited were struggling with this second phase—creating ongoing assessments and then using the results from those assessments for the third phase.

The third phase is targeted intervention. The most common of these was after-school tutoring programs. Although schools have offered after-school programs for some time, our sense was that they will become more effective as districts develop a better diagnostic tool for each student. In one high school, all students who had not reached a certain level on the SAT9 were required to attend 12 tutoring sessions specifically directed at areas on the exam in which they were struggling. This strategy seemed to be paying off because the school has consistently been in the top 10 percent in the Similar Schools Ranking. The superintendent of this district saw this kind of targeted intervention as a model of how his schools could improve most rapidly:

> If we had the money to pinpoint the needs of kids and really then get some quality tutoring on a small group basis, I think we could make faster progress.

Our visits lead us to believe that most districts share this vision: a good regular program that moves most students to proficiency, complemented by a series of targeted interventions to help students with specific gaps in their knowledge.

Conclusion

We found strong support among superintendents for California's standards-based reform. Although they pointed out many flaws in the way that reform was initially designed, superintendents endorsed the concept and seemed to believe that the state has steadily improved that design. In particular, superintendents did not view standards as an unwanted state intrusion into their districts' affairs. On this particular policy, they are willing agents eager to implement the state's vision.

Part of the reason that superintendents were so positive about standards is that the standards helped them assert their authority over what transpires in the classroom. Teachers necessarily lose some authority in the process. In one district we visited, some teachers were fighting back, claiming that state standards violated the academic freedom provisions in their contract. In most cases, however, teachers seemed to be working cooperatively with district leadership to implement the state's standards. Our survey revealed that teachers saw the standards as ambitious, as they certainly are, but few seemed to regard them as totally unreasonable.

Regarding the steps that their districts must go through to implement this vision, superintendents share a remarkably similar view: first, aligning curriculum with the state standards by adopting appropriate textbooks and establishing pacing calendars. After this initial phase, their focus seems to shift toward evaluating whether students are mastering those standards and devising intervention strategies for those who are not.

4. Student Achievement and Family Income

For its academic standards to be effective, a state must measure whether students are achieving those standards, and it must hold schools accountable for that achievement. California measures student achievement through a battery of standardized tests and the success of a school by its students' scores on those tests. These scores determine a school's API, and the goal for every school is an API of 800. Each year, a school is expected to make regular progress toward that goal.

As many studies have demonstrated, factors largely outside a school's control have a significant effect on student achievement. These factors include the education level of a student's parents, the involvement of those parents in their child's education, the language spoken in the student's home, and the environment in the student's neighborhood. In practice, many of these factors are strongly correlated with the income of a student's family, leading to a strong positive correlation between student achievement and family income.

This correlation creates a tension for any system of academic standards and school accountability. In the United States today, it is not politically tenable to have different expectations for students from different economic classes. Furthermore, to effect positive change, expectations should be high relative to current performance. Expectations high enough to be meaningful for most schools will be very difficult to meet in schools serving low-income students. As a consequence, an effective system of standards and accountability inevitably focuses attention on schools serving low-income students, even if those schools are doing their jobs very well. Meanwhile, schools in affluent areas escape serious examination even if they are not very effective. Holding all schools to the same achievement standard demands more from schools serving low-income students than it does from other schools. This chapter explores the resulting tension.

Family Income and the API

A school's API is strongly related to the socioeconomic status of its students. Figure 4.1 shows the API scores of California elementary schools plotted against the percentages of their students receiving free or reduced-price lunches. To be eligible for this program, the income of a student's family must be less than 185 percent of the poverty level; thus, eligibility measures the percentage of a school's students in low-income families. This percentage and the API numbers in Figure 4.1 are averages for the years 2001, 2002, and 2003. These three-year averages smooth out random, year-to-year variations, giving a more accurate picture of student background and achievement in a school. As the figure shows, the majority of schools in low-poverty neighborhoods achieve an 800 API, but very few achieve that goal in high-poverty neighborhoods. In fact, among the 752 elementary schools that have 90 percent or more of their students eligible for free or reduced-price lunches, none had an average API exceeding 800, and only 18 had an average exceeding 700. In contrast, among the 584 elementary schools with 10 percent or fewer students eligible for free or reduced-price

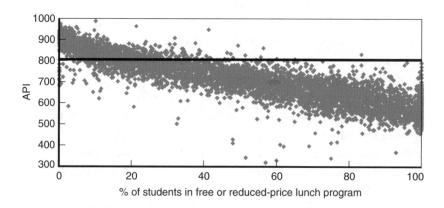

Figure 4.1—Elementary Schools, 2001–2003 Average

30

lunches, all but 36 had an API exceeding 800. A similar pattern holds for middle and high schools.

The relationship between family income and student achievement is surely due to many factors—one may be the lack of effectiveness of schools in low-income neighborhoods. However, we doubt that this is the primary factor because the connection between family income and achievement is so pervasive. The connection appears among students in the same school as well as across schools serving families of different income classes. A large part of the explanation of the relationship between income and achievement must therefore lie with factors associated with low-income families themselves, not the schools their children attend. Among those factors is the education level of a student's parents. Parents with little formal education may be less able to help their children with homework, less knowledgeable about the educational opportunities available to their children, and less effective in turning their high hopes for their children into reality. In California, many low-income families are also recent immigrants who speak a language other than English at home.

Our teacher survey suggests some factors that may explain the relationship between student achievement and family income. We asked teachers to rate the extent to which a variety of issues interfere with student achievement at their schools. Teachers were asked to rate these issues on a scale ranging from 1 to 5, where 1 indicates no interference and 5 indicates a great deal of interference. Table 4.1 lists the issues and shows the percentage of teachers answering 4 or 5, broken down by school level and SES.

According to the teachers in our sample, lack of student motivation, lack of parental support, inadequate English-language skills, and irregular student attendance posed a serious problem for student achievement at their schools. Between 45 and 60 percent of teachers rated these issues as a 4 or 5 on the scale.

Almost every issue caused more interference at low-SES schools than at high-SES schools. For example, although two-thirds of teachers from low-SES schools felt that students lacked parental support, only 18 percent of teachers from high-SES schools did. Although 56 percent

Table 4.1

Percentage of Teachers Rating Interference Level at 4 or 5, by School Type

Type of Interference	All	School Level			SES	
		Elem.	Middle	High	Low	High
Lack of student motivation	60	35	60	71	68	36
Lack of parental support	53	47	57	54	66	18
Lack of teacher training	8	7	8	9	10	4
Lack of school support programs	19	18	17	20	21	12
Too many students with inadequate English-language skills	45	46	43	45	56	13
Too many students with individual education plans	23	18	25	24	25	16
Student health problems	11	11	13	10	13	5
Irregular student attendance	49	28	44	61	59	22
Crime rate in school and surrounding areas	16	12	23	15	21	2

of teachers from low-SES schools cited language skills as a problem, just 13 percent of teachers from high-SES schools did so.

Teachers expanded on these responses in their answers to the open-ended question: "What are the two biggest challenges facing students at your school?" It is difficult to summarize the many responses we received to that question, but a simple comparison of responses from teachers at two elementary schools is a good beginning. One school is in an affluent suburb of one of California's largest cities. The school is nestled in a quiet neighborhood of townhouses and single-family homes and abuts a small city park. The building is relatively new, architecturally appealing, and well maintained. The principal of the school maintained that on any given day there were more volunteers at the school than paid staff.

In responding to our question, teachers in this school often expressed the concern that they were not sufficiently challenging the school's gifted students. Some also wrote that the high expectations of parents were a problem for some students. One teacher saw the biggest challenge for students as "pressure from parents to meet the level of other students." Another wrote that "students are expected to reach high to keep up with the other schools in our district." One teacher saw the biggest challenge facing students as "competition with each other." From 2001 through 2003, the school had an average API of nearly 900.

Compare these concerns with those of teachers at another elementary school in the same urban area. This school is in the area's inner city. Buildings in its neighborhood are marked with graffiti, the houses are small and poorly maintained, and the streets are full of litter. The school itself is a hodge-podge of portable classrooms and permanent structures built in different eras. The school has nearly 1,000 students, and the asphalt and dirt playground is cramped. The students are overwhelmingly from families who have recently emigrated from Mexico.

In their open-ended comments, teachers repeatedly identified learning English as the biggest challenge their students face. One teacher responded that "parents want their children to learn, but they cannot help because they don't have English literacy skills themselves." Another wrote that many parents have more than one job and that consequently "parent support with academic activities is not adequate." Another was concerned that students do not have a place to study at home that is clean and quiet.

The challenges facing new immigrants are obvious and daunting. But, some schools in low-income areas face challenges not related to the difficulties of learning a new language. One elementary school we visited is in a predominantly low-income neighborhood of an inner city. The residents are poor, but they are not immigrants. The school was recently renovated and adjoins a city park. It is not cramped or poorly maintained. It resembles schools one would expect to see in a middle-income suburb.

The teachers were very clear about the challenges their students faced. Over and over again, they mentioned the lack of positive role models for their students. One teacher wrote,

Many of our students are not motivated to succeed academically because their parents weren't successful in school.

Another expressed the challenge as not "seeing the future and the possibilities the world has for them." One wrote that the school's students were "living in an unstructured environment where they must act as the adult of the home."

These differences in teacher responses between schools in low-income areas and schools in more affluent areas are even clearer for high schools than for elementary schools. According to teachers at one affluent suburban high school we visited, it is a veritable pressure cooker. Physically, this school is unremarkable, with buildings crowded together on a campus that seems far too small for the number of students. Overwhelmingly, teachers saw their main challenge stemming from the tremendous pressure on students to excel. One teacher expressed the challenge students face as

> . . . balancing all they need to do. We are in a high-achieving, affluent community, and kids aim for the elite and upper-tier colleges. They have rigorous academic classes, school activities, and community service which they need to get into the top colleges. Many find it hard to fit it all in, especially since most have jobs also to pay for their car.

Many teachers in the school expressed concern over the lack of apparent options for students other than going to college. One teacher summarized the biggest challenge students face as "the realization that not all of them will be attending Stanford after graduation."

These concerns were very different from those of the teachers at a small, rural high school in the Central Valley. Many families in the area were recent immigrants and, although the school was small and welcoming, parents were not actively involved in their children's education. As one teacher wrote,

> Parents support education, but aren't sure what their role is in supporting their students.

Students also had few examples of adults who were highly educated and engaged in demanding and rewarding careers. According to one teacher, students lack motivation due to

> their inability to see a bright future. They see migrant work and drugs/gangs as their future.

Another teacher pointed to the competing demands on students' time because "a lot of students must work to help support their families."

There were many more responses from teachers that put the numbers in Table 4.1 into perspective. One came from a teacher in an inner-city middle school in a neighborhood rife with gang activity.

> Our parents are not well educated and were not successful in school themselves. They don't know how to help their kids. They don't understand a disciplined approach to studying and problem-solving.

A second was from a teacher in a high school located in a low-income suburban area.

> Many students lack motivation and hope for the future. I believe this behavior mirrors that of their parents or guardians, who accept "just getting by in life" by choice or by circumstances beyond their control.

As we emphasized above, it can be misleading to generalize from a few visits to a small number of schools. It may be even more misleading to generalize based on what a few teachers wrote in response to our survey. On the other hand, California is attempting to hold all public schools in the state to the same high standards, a considerable generalization itself. In pursuing that objective, it is sometimes easy to forget the vastly different environments in which children live. The few examples we have highlighted serve to remind us of these differences. Although they are not proof of a general proposition, they are counterexamples to the proposition that all schools have essentially the same job to do.

Has California Set the Bar Too High?

The superintendents we visited were keenly aware of the relationship between student achievement and family and were fully cognizant that the state's high achievement goal would be difficult for schools in low-income areas. The superintendent of a district in an affluent suburban area was quick to point out that the high APIs (all over 800) of schools in his district were not a fair measure of the effectiveness of those schools. He attributed those scores as much to the influence of the district's parents as to the work of his own teachers, principals, and other staff. Another superintendent in a large central city district referred to the API as the "Affluent Parent Index."

We observed above how rare it is for a school to reach 800 if it has a high concentration of poor students. This observation leads naturally to the question of whether California has set its performance goal too high. The superintendent of a large urban district responded:

> While 800 was established as the goal toward which schools ought to be headed, five percent growth toward that target was the thing that made all the practitioners breath a sigh of relief and say, "You know what? If that's really how they're going to look at schools, we can handle that." From the urban areas, I don't think there was a lot of expectation that a lot of schools would be someday getting to 800.

The difficulty with that sigh of relief is that it is only temporary. If the maximum API a school can reach is 650, for example, it can only grow so long at 5 percent per year before it hits its maximum. Indeed, two schools we visited seemed to be struggling with this issue. One was an elementary school and the other a high school. Both had experienced rapid growth in their APIs and both were in the top 10 percent of their 100 Similar Schools. Yet both were beginning to experience diminishing returns. The strategies that had yielded rapid growth in test scores seemed to have run their course, and both schools were searching for new strategies that would take them to a higher level of achievement.

The experiences of these schools highlight a deep concern about setting a high performance goal for all schools. Without a large infusion of resources to low-income schools, is it really possible to close the achievement gap between those schools and schools in more affluent neighborhoods? Our accountability system may only be spotlighting a problem that California does not have the political will to remedy. A superintendent of a large, diverse suburban district pointed directly to that issue:

> We've got kids whose parents are professors at the university in town, and we've got kids who were just evicted from a motel. They were living in absolute filth, two families to a motel room. So I think that society is going to have to recognize that without some kind of major league help for these kids to overcome these obstacles, we're going to have a major schism in California education that is going to be pretty much down that line of poverty.

Federal Standards

The federal No Child Left Behind (NCLB) legislation focuses even more attention on this issue. Under that legislation, 100 percent of students in a school must be "proficient" by 2014. Each state is required to establish its own definition of proficiency, and California had already established a very high standard. In terms of API scores, proficiency is 875, which is well above the median performance of students in the rest of the nation. But it is not just that students in a school must average 875. By 2014, all students in a school must have a score of 875 or above. Many fear that this extremely high performance standard may undermine support for the general concept of standards and accountability. We heard early worries about this unfortunate possibility from the superintendents we interviewed. One said,

> Until No Child Left Behind, we thought, well, we're going to be behind this and make this work, but we're having some different thoughts at this point. We certainly promote the whole notion of having the highest of standards for kids, but when you get into the practicality of holding every single student, no matter what their background is, accountable for those high standards, it's more than just difficult.

In fact, 100 percent proficiency is "more than just difficult," it is literally impossible. As long as proficiency is determined by a standardized test in which students bubble in the answers to multiple choice questions, some scores will fall below any set standard, even if all students are actually proficient. Test results are a statistic, not a perfect measure of knowledge or accomplishment. Like many statistics, test scores involve a significant error component. California's API reduces that error because it averages test scores across students in a school. Although this averaging means that a school may be deemed successful even though some students are not proficient, it greatly reduces the risk that a school will be labeled underperforming when all of its students are in fact proficient. In a statistical sense, this average balances two potential types of error. One type of error is labeling a school underperforming when its students are all proficient. Another is declaring that a school is meeting performance goals when many of its students are not proficient. An average strikes a balance between those two types of errors. No Child Left Behind minimizes the second type of error at the expense of greatly increasing the first type. This problem will become evident in 2014 when all American public schools will be labeled underperforming by the NCLB measure. In the meantime, more and more schools will be labeled underperforming each year, raising concerns about the concept of school accountability.

California has exacerbated this problem by setting a very high standard for proficiency. California's high standards for proficiency are not really the problem, however. No proficiency standard is low enough to make 100 percent proficiency feasible. The problem is the requirement that all students be proficient, not the proficiency standard itself.

Conclusion

The laudable goal of setting high standards for all students inevitably focuses attention on the difference in achievement among students from different economic classes. Schools may be part of the explanation for this difference, but we doubt that they are the most important. Within the same classrooms, students from low-income families tend to achieve less academically than children from high-income families. If income matters within classrooms and schools, it surely matters across schools, explaining much of the remarkably consistent link between poverty and API shown in Figure 4.1.

Family income may have a direct effect on a student's performance in school, and it may also serve as a proxy for other factors that may affect a student's performance. As examples of direct effects, low-income families cannot afford tutors when their children struggle with schoolwork and may not even be able to provide them a quiet place to study at home. In these two examples, the lack of family resources may inhibit student performance. However, family income may also be a proxy for other complicated factors that affect student achievement. A family in which the parents are poorly educated may struggle to make a reasonable income and may also be poorly equipped to help its children with regular homework. A family caught up in drugs and crime may struggle in all aspects of life, including earning a living and educating children. In contrast, a family led by ambitious and disciplined parents is likely to be successful economically and educationally.

The distinction between income as a proxy and income as a direct effect has important policy implications. To the extent that income is mainly a proxy, schools serving low-income students face an uphill battle. To the extent that income has a direct effect on educational outcomes, schools may be successful in improving achievement among low-income students by providing many of the extra resources that higher-income families would provide to their children. An effective after-school tutoring program could substitute for tutors that a more affluent family would provide. An extended school day or school year could have the same effect.

This issue of school resources and student poverty is the next logical phase of the movement for standards and accountability. The problem of imposing high expectations on all students has focused attention on the differences in student achievement among students from different economic classes. The question now is whether additional resources for schools serving low-income students can help close that gap. The answer is assuredly affirmative, although the real questions are these: How much in additional resources are needed, what kind of resources are required, and are we willing to make that kind of expenditure? The next chapter explores some of this terrain by examining what resource differences currently exist among the schools we visited.

5. School Resources and Student Poverty

The link between poverty and academic achievement is strong and persistent. As the last chapter revealed, this link is very clear when the API scores of California schools are plotted against the percentage of students in those schools from low-income families. Schools with many low-income students have considerably lower API scores than schools with more affluent students. This link suggests that low-SES schools may need more resources than high-SES schools if they are to meet the state's high expectations.

Yet, as *High Expectations, Modest Means* demonstrated, school districts with high percentages of low-income students do receive more revenue per pupil than other schools. A district with a high percentage of low-income students may receive more revenue per pupil than other districts, but does that mean that the high-poverty schools in such a district receive more resources than the low-poverty schools? Ultimately, a popularly elected school board decides how to allocate unrestricted revenue across schools in its district. Because most of a school district's revenue is unrestricted and because the board must be sensitive to the concerns of local parents, it seems possible that the board could still try to equalize per-pupil resources within the district.

This chapter compares resource levels between the high- and low-SES schools that we visited. We base this comparison on financial data we gathered from the school district. We supplement this financial picture of day-to-day operations with the teachers' views on the adequacy of their facilities, as well as on our own impressions of the physical condition of the schools during our visits.

School Expenditures

School districts receive revenues from a variety of sources, which can be divided into four main categories: revenue limit funds, state categorical funds, federal categorical funds, and local funds. Revenue limit funds constitute about two-thirds of all districts' general fund revenue and are primarily made up of state aid and ad valorem property taxes. Local funds include revenues from local sources other than the ad valorem property tax, such as interest, rentals, and parcel taxes. Revenue limit funds and most local funds are unrestricted in the sense that they can be used for any legitimate purpose determined by the school district governing board. The state has nearly equalized per-pupil revenue limit funds at the district level. In contrast, state and federal categorical funds are targeted to particular programs or populations of students. The two largest categorical programs are special education for the disabled (funded jointly by state and federal funds) and the state K–3 class size reduction (K–3 CSR) program.

Certain categorical programs target students from low-income families and are called compensatory programs. The two largest such programs are the state Economic Impact Aid program and the federal Title I program. The compensatory revenue that a district receives is strongly related to the percentage of its students who are from low-income families. Because compensatory funds are earmarked for low-income students, one would expect that schools serving low-income students would spend more from compensatory funds than do schools serving higher-income students. Does this trend imply that schools with high percentages of low-income students have higher levels of total expenditures per pupil than do schools with lower percentages of students in poverty? Or would districts offset increases in compensatory funds with fewer unrestricted funds, so that school resources were the same throughout a district regardless of student income?

To answer these questions, we compare mean expenditures per pupil from these categories for low-SES and high-SES schools. The expenditure data for the schools came from the school district financial offices. Although districts report their financial data to the state at the district level using the Standardized Account Code Structure (SACS), many districts actually track expenditures to the school site. We designed a method to gather consistent, comparable data traced to the school site and worked closely with district financial offices to gather these data. We were able to obtain financial data for 41 of the 49 schools we visited. Appendix C describes the SACS data and our method of categorizing expenditures. Because this study is the first to gather financial data at the school level in California, the appendix also provides additional analyses of school expenditures. In this chapter, we focus on expenditures at the school site level that are essential for the day-to-day operations of the school. We exclude the school's share of district-level expenditures, such as superintendent's salary, testing costs, and transportation costs. (See Appendix C for a complete list of district-level expenditures.) We group most expenditures into categories based on whether they come from restricted or unrestricted sources, but we separate expenditures for maintenance and operations regardless of the funding source.

Tables 5.1 through 5.3 compare mean spending per pupil between low-SES and high-SES elementary, middle, and high schools, respectively. As expected, the relationship between compensatory spending and student poverty holds for the schools in our sample, with low-SES schools spending more from compensatory sources. This relationship is more pronounced for elementary and middle schools than for high schools.

For elementary schools, on average, the eight low-SES schools we visited spent $431 more compensatory funds per pupil than did the six high-SES schools—$454 versus $23 (see Table 5.1). These low-SES schools also spent $354 per pupil more from other state and federal categorical funds and $130 more on maintenance and operations than did high-SES schools. The higher level of categorical spending at low-SES schools was largely offset by lower spending levels from unrestricted sources. On average, low-SES elementary schools spent $788 per pupil, or 17.9 percent, less from unrestricted funds than did the high-SES schools. In total, the low-SES elementary schools spent just $13 more per pupil than did the high-SES schools.

Table 5.1

School Site Spending per Pupil, by Program: Elementary Schools
(in $)

Category	High-SES	Low-SES	Difference, Low – High
Unrestricted	4,409	3,621	–788
Compensatory education	23	454	431
Special education	687	603	–84
Other categorical	376	730	354
Local restricted	142	112	–30
Maintenance and operations	476	606	130
Total	6,113	6,126	13

A similar trend holds for middle schools, although total spending per pupil was significantly higher for the 10 low-SES schools than for the three high-SES schools. As Table 5.2 shows, low-SES middle schools spent on average $368 per pupil more from compensatory funds than did the high-SES schools. The low-SES schools also spent $258 per pupil more from other state and federal categorical funds and $94 per pupil more on maintenance and operations. In terms of unrestricted funds, however, the low-SES middle schools spent $584 less per pupil than did the high-SES middle schools. In total, the low-SES middle

Table 5.2

School Site Spending per Pupil, by Program: Middle Schools
(in $)

Category	High-SES	Low-SES	Difference, Low – High
Unrestricted	4,283	3,699	–584
Compensatory education	28	396	368
Special education	741	740	–1
Other categorical	424	682	258
Local restricted	14	71	57
Maintenance and operations	531	625	94
Total	6,021	6,213	192

schools spent $192 more per pupil than did the high-SES middle schools.

Like the elementary and middle schools, the 11 low-SES high schools we visited spent more from compensatory funds, as well as from other state and federal categorical programs, than the three high-SES schools (Table 5.3). Unlike the lower school levels, however, the low- and high-SES high schools spent virtually the same amount per pupil from unrestricted sources—$4,151 versus $4,169. In total, the low-SES high schools' spending per pupil exceeded that of high-SES schools by $541.

Low-SES schools spent more per pupil in total than did high-SES schools but not always by as much as the compensatory education funds would suggest. Low-SES schools did receive more compensatory revenue per pupil than did high-SES schools. However, for the elementary and middle schools we visited, these additional resources were completely offset by lower levels of unrestricted funds.

Although California has pursued a policy of equalizing unrestricted revenue among school districts, there is no requirement that school districts allocate these unrestricted funds equally to their schools. But why should the elementary and middle schools in our sample that serve students from low-income families spend less in unrestricted funding per pupil than schools serving students from higher-income families? Does

Table 5.3

School Site Spending per Pupil, by Program: High Schools
(in $)

Category	High-SES	Low-SES	Difference, Low – High
Unrestricted	4,169	4,151	−18
Compensatory education	18	206	188
Special education	768	769	1
Other categorical	526	720	194
Local restricted	45	61	16
Maintenance and operations	567	727	160
Total	6,093	6,634	541

spending less from unrestricted funds actually translate into fewer tangible resources?

Roza and Hill (2003) suggest that a large part of the spending difference in unrestricted funds may arise because districts attempt to equalize the teacher-pupil ratio across schools rather than to equalize compensation per teacher. Under collective bargaining agreements, teachers with greater experience typically have more influence over where they teach, with the more experienced teachers tending to avoid low-SES schools. Taken together, schools serving low-SES students have the same number of teachers per pupil but tend to get the newer, less experienced teachers. Because less experienced teachers are paid less, low-SES schools tend to spend less from unrestricted funds for teacher salaries. A recent study estimated the difference in average teacher salary between high- and low-SES schools in the same district and found that average salaries do tend to be lower in low-SES schools (The Education Trust-West, 2005). Can these differences explain the difference in unrestricted funding per pupil we observe in our sample of schools?

Our data allow us to address this question directly by separating unrestricted expenditures into expenditures on teachers' salaries and expenditures on everything else. As Table 5.4 shows, high-SES schools in our sample do spend more unrestricted funds per pupil on teachers

Table 5.4

Unrestricted Spending per Pupil
(in $)

School Level	Teachers	Other	Total
Elementary schools			
High-SES	2,570	1,839	4,409
Low-SES	1,973	1,648	3,621
Middle schools			
High-SES	2,111	2,172	4,283
Low-SES	1,904	1,795	3,699
High schools			
High-SES	2,311	1,858	4,169
Low-SES	2,225	1,926	4,151

than do low-SES schools. For example, the high-SES elementary schools we visited spent an average of $2,570 per pupil on teachers—$597 more than the $1,973 spent at low-SES elementary schools. For middle and high schools, the same general pattern holds, although the differences in teacher spending per pupil are less than half as large as for elementary schools. High-SES middle schools spent $207 more and high-SES high schools spent $86 more than their low-SES counterparts.

Expenditures on teachers are not the only source of differences in unrestricted spending per pupil. As Table 5.4 also reveals, for elementary and middle schools, unrestricted expenditures on goods and services other than teacher salaries are higher for high-SES schools than for low-SES schools. High schools are an exception; nonteacher expenditures per pupil are slightly higher for the low-SES schools.

Differences in teacher spending per pupil could arise from two sources: differences in average salary per teacher and differences in the number of teachers per pupil. Table 5.5 shows both sources are at work for elementary and middle schools. For elementary schools, the average salary per teacher is $57,242 for high-SES schools and $47,545 for low-SES schools. This difference also exists for middle and high schools, although the magnitude of the difference is considerably smaller. For

Table 5.5

Components of Teacher Expenditures

School Level	Average Teacher Salary ($)	Teachers per 1,000 Students
Elementary schools		
High-SES	57,242	44.9
Low-SES	47,545	41.5
Middle schools		
High-SES	56,089	37.6
Low-SES	53,422	35.6
High schools		
High-SES	64,623	35.8
Low-SES	61,410	36.2

elementary schools, the difference was almost $10,000. For middle and high schools, the difference was approximately $3,000.

Teacher-pupil ratios largely reinforce the expenditure differences that result from differences in average salaries. As Table 5.5 shows, high-SES elementary and middle schools had more teachers per pupil than did their low-SES counterparts. However, this pattern was not true for high schools. The high-SES high schools we visited had slightly fewer teachers per pupil than did the low-SES high schools we visited.

Both sources—average teacher salary and teacher-pupil ratios— contribute to the difference in teacher expenditures from unrestricted revenue. In general, average teacher salary is a more important source. To see this, we broke down the difference in average spending per pupil on teachers into two parts: spending per pupil if the cost per teacher was different but the pupil-teacher ratio was the same, and spending per pupil if the teacher-pupil ratio was different but the cost per teacher was the same. The results are displayed in Table 5.6. For elementary schools, the difference in the average teacher's salary explains 70 percent of the difference in teacher spending per pupil. For middle schools, it explains 47 percent. For high schools, the entire difference is due to average teacher salary. The teacher-pupil ratio actually works in the opposite direction, offsetting differences in teacher spending that result from the higher salaries in high-SES schools.

In sum, a large part of the difference in unrestricted spending can be explained by differences in teacher salary rather than differences in staffing levels. However, spending less on teachers but getting the same number of teachers with slightly less experience may not reflect a true

Table 5.6

Sources of Differences Between Low-Poverty and High-Poverty Schools in Teacher Expenditures per Pupil

School Level	% of Difference Due to:	
	Average Teacher Salary	Teachers per 1,000 Students
Elementary schools	70	30
Middle schools	47	53
High schools	134	–34

resource difference. Rivkin, Hanushek, and Kain (2005) quantify teacher quality based on whether a teacher has been able to increase the academic achievement of his or her students. Teachers with more than three years of experience are more effective on average than teachers with less experience. However, experience beyond three years does not appear to have a positive effect on average teacher effectiveness. Furthermore, formal education beyond the credential has no significant influence. Therefore, differences in unrestricted funds resulting from differences in teacher education and experience may not accurately reflect real resource differences.

Classrooms and Textbooks

Whereas our budget data allow us to compare the resource levels of day-to-day expenditures, we relied on our teacher survey to paint a picture of two important physical aspects of schools: the condition of classrooms and the availability of textbooks. These two aspects of education are an integral part of the daily learning environment for students and the working conditions for teachers.

We asked teachers to rate the quality of several classroom features: the room itself (ceiling, walls, floor, and door), student desks, lighting, and windows. They could rate the quality as poor, fair, good, or excellent. Table 5.7 shows the percentage of teachers, broken down by school level and SES, who rated the given classroom conditions as poor. The differences by school level are small, except in the area of student desks. Fifteen percent of high school teachers said that student desks in their classroom were in poor condition, compared to 8 to 9 percent of elementary and middle school teachers.

Table 5.7

Percentage of Teachers Rating a Classroom Condition as Poor

| Classroom Feature | All | School Level | | | SES | |
		Elem.	Middle	High	Low	High
Ceiling, walls, floor, and door	12	11	10	13	13	8
Student desks	12	8	9	15	14	4
Lighting	6	6	6	6	6	5
Windows	15	14	15	16	17	10

Classroom conditions were generally worse in the low-SES schools than in the high-SES schools. For example, 13 percent of teachers in the low-SES schools rated the room itself as being in poor condition, compared to only 8 percent of teachers in the high-SES schools. Seventeen percent of teachers in low-SES schools rated the windows as poor, compared to only 10 percent in the high-SES schools. Despite these differences based on SES, even the percentage of teachers reporting poor conditions in low-SES schools is small compared to the widespread image of dilapidated buildings sometimes portrayed in the media.

We also asked teachers which aspects of their physical environment interfered with student learning in their classroom. Their answers appear in Table 5.8. About 8 percent of teachers reported that they did not have enough desks for all their students, yet this deficiency occurred at middle and high schools and not elementary schools. The prevalence of this problem appears unrelated to the SES of the school. Of those teachers lacking desks, half were missing desks for at least 5 percent of their students, and one-quarter were missing desks for at least 10 percent of their students.

Nearly one-third of teachers indicated that the noise level of the surrounding environment posed a problem for student learning. Teachers at low-SES schools were more likely than teachers at high-SES schools to complain of noisy surroundings. Forty-two percent of teachers indicated that extreme classroom temperatures interfered with classroom learning. High school teachers reported this problem at a

Table 5.8

Percentage of Teachers Indicating That the Following Issues Interfere with Student Learning in Their Classroom

		School Level			SES	
Problem	All	Elem.	Middle	High	Low	High
Not enough desks for all students	8	1	10	11	9	7
Noise level of surrounding environment	30	30	27	32	33	21
Uncomfortably hot or cold temperature in classroom	42	34	37	48	41	45

slightly higher rate than did elementary and middle school teachers, but there was little difference based on the SES of the school.

Another important classroom issue is the condition and availability of textbooks. Categorical programs in the past have earmarked money explicitly for instructional materials such as textbooks. Yet, issues such as inadequate numbers or poor quality of textbooks are still often at the heart of the debate when it comes to adequate resources. Accordingly, we asked our teachers a series of questions about textbooks—whether they had enough for every student to use a copy in the classroom, whether they had enough for every student to take a copy home, and whether their students all had the same edition of the textbooks. Table 5.9 shows how teachers responded to these questions.

About 18 percent of teachers reported that not every student had a textbook to use in the classroom. The problem was more severe in middle and high schools and in low-SES schools. For those teachers who indicated that they lacked books for all their students, we followed up with a question about how many students were missing books. When elementary and middle school teachers were missing books, they generally were missing books for about one-quarter of their class. When high school teachers were missing books, they were missing books for about half of their students.

A more prevalent problem than missing books for classroom use was the problem of lacking books for students to take home. Nearly 30 percent of teachers reported that not every student had a copy of their

Table 5.9

Percentage of Teachers Indicating Problems with Availability of Textbooks

		School Level			SES	
Problem	All	Elem.	Middle	High	Low	High
Not enough textbooks for classroom	18	11	17	22	21	12
Not enough textbooks for student to take copy home	29	20	33	31	33	17
Different textbook editions interfere with teaching	3	2	3	3	3	2

textbook to take home. Lacking textbooks for home use was more of a problem at middle and high schools and slightly more of a problem at low-SES schools than at high-SES schools. Regardless of the school level or SES, not many teachers indicated that having different editions of textbooks interfered with their teaching.

Of the textbooks teachers did use for their classes, most were relatively new. Having newer textbooks is an important part of aligning a school's curriculum to the state standards. As Table 5.10 shows, close to 70 percent of teachers used textbooks less than five years old. High schools teachers were less likely than middle and elementary school teachers to have new textbooks. Teachers is low-SES schools were more likely to have the newest textbooks, yet the percentage of teachers with textbooks more than eight years old did not differ based on the school's SES.

Table 5.10

Age of Most Frequently Used Textbooks
(Percentage Distribution)

Age	All	School Level			SES	
		Elem.	Middle	High	Low	High
Less than 2 years	36	48	44	26	38	29
2–4 years	32	32	28	35	32	35
5–8 years	12	7	6	16	11	14
More than 8 years	6	2	3	9	6	6
Does not apply	12	10	16	12	12	15
Missing	2	2	2	2	2	2

First Impressions

The responses to our survey provide some information about the condition of school facilities, particularly classrooms. To supplement that information, we also conducted a quick inspection of the buildings and grounds of each school we visited. This inspection was not meant to address fundamental questions such as the soundness of the structures or the adequacy of the science labs. Our inspection was more impressionistic than fundamental. Is the paint fresh, are any windows broken, are the grounds well maintained, are the lavatories clean, is graffiti visible? In the process, we also formed overall impressions of the physical condition of each school, impressions that are difficult to quantify but easy to describe. Although these impressions are far from scientific and we would not want anyone to generalize from them, we have been asked many times to describe what we saw. This short section is our response.

It is easier to describe what we did not see. We did not see broken windows, graffiti, or large areas of peeling paint. A few buildings had small areas of peeling paint under eaves or on door frames, but these were relatively minor. One school building had a small bit of graffiti from the night before, but the maintenance staff was removing it as we visited. Litter was another issue. Although we did not see much litter on the grounds of elementary schools, we saw plenty at middle and high schools.

The newest of the schools we visited were all in relatively affluent areas. They were all very attractive, but two stood out. One blended traditional school design with some modern touches to give a warm, welcoming feeling. Another was strikingly modern. It had also been designed with careful attention to function. The principal had worked closely with the architect to get the features that he wanted his school to have. It was literally a school designed around an educational plan.

Schools in less affluent areas were older and generally less attractive. In several cases, we found a fine old building fenced in by boxy portables. The portables served very well as classrooms, and the principals told us that teachers often preferred the portables to classrooms in the main building. However, architecturally, the portables detracted from the main building and took up valuable playground space. In one elementary school, the playground space was so limited that recess ran in shifts.

We discovered three old gems in our visits to less affluent areas, however. All were mission style buildings with red tile roofs and smooth stucco walls. One old high school, built in the 1920s and recently remodeled, had beautiful interior woodwork. One middle school boasted an interior courtyard and arched walkways. It also adjoined a beautiful city park.

A few schools we visited were old and tired. Three were in a low-income, desert town. The buildings were clean but old and needing repair. In one school, a building had been condemned and was not being used. A beautiful new science building had just being completed, however. In all three schools, the playgrounds had cracked asphalt and uneven surfaces.

The majority of our schools fell between these two extremes. Many were built in the 1960s and 1970s. They were generally low-slung and undistinguished. Many had been recently renovated, and some were scheduled for renovation. All of these schools were functional. They were not something that a community would necessarily point to with pride, but they were not embarrassments, either.

One high school we visited was also built in the 1960s and was undistinguished architecturally. It stood out, however, because of the exceptional effort the district put into maintaining it. Litter was picked up every morning and also throughout the day. The district renovated a few classrooms every year, rather than waiting until all of them needed fresh paint and new desks. There was a sense of planning and pride in the maintenance of this school that was not evident in many others. The school was located in a low-income area and compared very favorably to the high schools in our two most affluent areas.

Given the variety of schools we visited, it is difficult to generalize about the relationship between the physical condition of schools and the SES of a school's students. Nevertheless, among our 49 schools, the four that were in the most obvious need of renovation were all serving low-income students. At the other end of the spectrum, the five newest schools we visited were all in relatively affluent neighborhoods. However, not all schools in affluent neighborhoods were new and several were quite undistinguished. Furthermore, several older schools, including three real classics, were very well maintained and very attractive. On balance, the schools in affluent areas seemed in better condition than other schools, but there were many exceptions to this general trend.

Conclusion

Given that low-SES schools are furthest from the state's API goals and may ultimately need more resources for their students to meet the state's standards, it is important to take stock of their current resource levels. The low-SES schools we visited currently receive and spend more from compensatory funding programs. Compared to their high-SES counterparts, low-SES elementary schools spent $431 per pupil more on average, low-SES middle schools spent $368 per pupil more, and low-SES high schools spent $188 per pupil more from compensatory sources. In elementary and middle schools, however, these higher levels of compensatory funding among low-SES schools were more than offset by lower levels of unrestricted funding. This lower level of unrestricted funding is partly due to differences among teacher salaries and, to a lesser extent, to differences in the teacher staffing levels.

The results from our teacher survey suggest that the physical condition of classrooms is generally acceptable. Our own impressions of the schools echo that sentiment. Only 12 percent of teachers rated the condition of their classrooms as poor. However, 30 percent of teachers reported that the noise level of the surrounding environment interfered with student learning and 42 percent of teachers reported that uncomfortable classroom temperatures interfered. Perceptions of resource adequacy did not vary substantially with the SES of schools. The noise level was a slightly bigger problem in low-SES schools, but temperature was a bigger issue in high-SES schools. The needs of elementary, middle, and high schools, however, are quite different. The availability of textbooks and desks was a bigger issue in middle and high schools than in elementary schools.

Given the small number of schools we visited, our results should be regarded as suggestive rather than definitive. Geographic differences in wages and costs may explain some of the spending patterns we observe. With only 41 schools providing finance data, we cannot simultaneously control for all these factors. Nevertheless, our examination is noteworthy because it is the first time that consistent, comparable data on school resources have been traced to the site level in California. The method we developed and the analyses presented herein are applicable to much larger samples of California schools; they thus point the way toward a better understanding of how resources are deployed at the school site level.

6. What Do Schools Need?

The previous chapter examined the budgets of the schools we visited, leading naturally to the question of what resources schools need to meet the state's expectations for them. This is the right question to ask and extremely important for public policy, but it is also ill-defined. Many resources would help schools. But resources also have prices, and the state has many demands on its limited budget. That is why we attempted to establish some realistic boundaries before we asked the principals of these schools in a previous report what resources were needed. We asked them to consider two hypothetical schools, one with a more advantaged student body than the other. For each school, we gave principals a budget and prices for various school resources and then asked them what resources they would employ and what they could achieve with those resources. We started with a budget roughly consistent with the resources California schools currently have. We then asked principals what additional resources they would employ if we increased their budgets by 15 percent. We repeated that exercise with a 30 percent increase. Their answers are summarized in Rose, Sonstelie, and Richardson (2004).

This chapter supplements those answers with the views of teachers and superintendents—teachers in the schools we visited and superintendents of their school districts. In our survey of teachers, we asked respondents to identify areas in their schools that were currently understaffed. In our interviews with superintendents, we asked how they would allocate an additional $500 per pupil in permanent, unrestricted funds. Our survey of teachers did not impose the budget constraints central to the budget simulations with principals. Although the question we posed to superintendents was more specific about budgets, we did not ask them for the specific answers principals provided. Despite these limitations, the responses of teachers and superintendents help fill in the picture of what educators in California believe their schools need to be successful.

School Staffing Levels

The opinions of teachers about staffing levels are easier to appreciate when the subject is placed in the context of staffing levels in other states. To facilitate these comparisons, we express staffing levels in terms of staff full-time-equivalents per pupil. In 2001–2002, staffing levels in California schools were 72 percent of the staffing levels in all other states (Rose et al., 2003). For teachers and instructional aides, these percentages were 75 percent and 80 percent. The percentages were considerably lower for counselors and librarians—46 percent and 38 percent. Administrative categories fared somewhat better—60 percent for administrators and 103 percent for administrative support. In addition to these well-defined categories, school districts employ many other staff members, including janitors, school nurses, security guards, computer support staff, and so on. In this diverse category, which constitutes about 30 percent of school district staff, the ratio of staff to students in California was 58 percent of the ratio in other states.

In light of these comparisons, it is understandable that teachers in California schools might feel that their staffing levels are inadequate. We found this attitude to be generally true, although not in every area. We asked teachers in the schools we visited whether staffing levels in their schools were adequate in the 12 areas listed in Table 6.1. About 40 percent of teachers indicated an inadequate level of staff for social and behavior counseling services as well as for health services and technology support. In contrast, most teachers responded that staffing was adequate in the areas of administrative support, school leadership, and library.

Elementary school teachers responded quite differently from teachers at middle and high school. For example, elementary school teachers were more likely to report inadequate levels of language learning support staff. About one-quarter of middle and high school teachers perceived a need for language support, but more than 40 percent of elementary schools teachers did. In almost every staffing area, elementary school teachers more frequently reported inadequate staffing levels. This deficiency raises the question of whether the reduced class sizes in

Table 6.1

Percentage of Teachers Thinking Staffing Level in the Following Areas Is Inadequate

Staffing Area	All	School Level			SES	
		Elem.	Middle	High	Low	High
Administrative office support	12	9	12	13	14	7
Counseling services—academic	32	46	31	26	33	29
Counseling services—social	41	50	38	39	42	37
Custodial/maintenance	30	25	24	35	31	29
Health (school nurse)	40	37	37	43	37	47
Language learning support	30	41	24	28	29	35
Library	16	17	16	15	17	12
Music/art/drama	30	66	32	13	31	28
School leadership (principal, vice principal)	9	7	8	11	11	5
Security (guards, police)	32	48	28	27	34	27
Speech/language therapy	20	26	17	20	23	14
Technology support	38	43	38	36	38	38

elementary schools, resulting from the state's K–3 CSR program, have come at the expense of staffing in other key areas.

Teacher responses did not vary much with the socioeconomic status of schools. Teachers in low-SES schools were more likely to respond that staffing was inadequate in the areas of administration, counseling, security, and speech. On the other hand, they were less likely to find staffing inadequate in the areas of health and language learning support. In all cases, these differences were relatively small.

We did not ask teachers to indicate directly whether their school had an adequate number of teachers and instructional aides. In their written responses to open-ended questions, however, many teachers complained about the size of their classes. These complaints were particularly prevalent among high school teachers, who can have five classes a day with more than 30 students in each class. With this many students, grading homework assignments and quizzes is a time-consuming task. As a consequence, teachers may be inclined to assign less homework and give fewer quizzes than they should. Teachers often pointed out this unfortunate consequence of large classes.

Professional Development

Despite the relatively low staffing levels in their schools, superintendents did not generally focus on staffing when we asked them what they would do with an additional $500 per student. That could be due to the relatively small increase we proposed. Five hundred dollars per pupil is less than 10 percent of a typical district's operating budget. On the other hand, assuming salary and benefits for a teacher at $60,000 per year, an extra $500 per student could reduce class sizes from 30 to 24 students per class. In any event, in response to this question, most superintendents emphasized increasing the effectiveness of the staff they had rather than increasing the number of staff. Ten out of 19 superintendents answered that they would allocate at least some part of those funds to professional development activities oriented around collective efforts to enhance student achievement. One superintendent described the need this way:

> We're always struggling with time and people, and not having enough to do those things that need to be done. If you don't get the information to teachers in a way they can use it, quickly and efficiently, they won't use it, because they're busy trying to figure out how to get from day to day.

We saw this struggle constantly when we visited schools. Schools had very little time to set aside for in-depth analysis, discussion, or reflection. Time to work on pacing calendars, analyze test data, and discuss instructional strategies was wedged in here and there during a school day, and these meetings often seemed haphazard and rushed.

In the budget simulations in our earlier report, principals also emphasized the importance of professional development. Principals had a baseline allocation of 14 hours of professional teacher development per year as part of the standard contract for teachers. They were able to add additional hours but were required to compensate teachers for this additional time. For the low-SES schools with the smallest budget, elementary school principals added an average of 33 hours of professional development a year. With the largest budgets, that total increased to 51 hours, a 55 percent increase. For the middle schools, principals added an average of 31 hours with the lowest budget and an average of 49 hours with the highest budget, a 58 percent increase. For the high schools, the increase was 68 percent, from 40 hours to 67 hours. Results were similar for the high-SES school.

Contrast these responses with the responses teachers gave to survey questions about professional development (Table 6.2). In one question, teachers were asked to report the number of hours they spent in the prior year on "professional development activities." They were asked to include all time, regardless of whether they were reimbursed by their school district. The median response to this question was 40 hours per year. A little less than half of that time was geared toward discussions or planning for the state standards. Remarkably, that median was the same for all school levels and for teachers at either low-SES or high-SES schools. This median was significantly lower than the average number of professional development hours that principals chose in the lowest budget scenario.

The goal of professional development is to prepare teachers to educate their students. In California, this goal now has a fairly precise definition—the state's academic content standards. We asked teachers how prepared they thought they were to teach all their students to those standards. Most teachers believed that they were well prepared (Table 6.3). Regardless of school level or SES of their school, 60 percent of teachers felt very well prepared to teach their students to the state standards. On the other hand, more than 30 percent of teachers believed that they were not well prepared.

Table 6.2

Median Hours of Professional Development Last School Year

		School Level			SES	
	All	Elem.	Middle	High	Low	High
Professional development hours	40	40	40	40	40	40
Hours geared toward standards	18	21	18	15	20	15

Table 6.3

How Prepared Teachers Feel to Teach All Their Students to the State Standards (Percentage Distribution)

| | All | School Level | | | SES | |
		Elem.	Middle	High	Low	High
Very well prepared	61	62	60	62	61	62
Only somewhat prepared	29	33	30	27	29	29
Not very well prepared	3	2	4	3	4	1
Does not apply/missing	7	3	6	8	6	8

As expected, the teachers who were new to the profession were more likely to indicate that they were not fully prepared. Among teachers with fewer than five years of experience, only 55 percent believed that they were very well prepared (Table 6.4). In contrast, among teachers with 10 or more years of experience, 66 percent believed they were very well prepared to teach. Perhaps it is the inexperienced teachers whom principals had in mind when they allocated substantial additional funds to professional development as their budgets increased.

Many schools now regard professional development as an ongoing process, which engages even the most experienced, educated, and accomplished teachers. Professional development certainly includes training in pedagogical techniques, which is the training that is most valuable to inexperienced teachers. We discovered, however, that professional development more often means a collaboration among teachers and administrators that focuses on developing strategies for enhancing student achievement. These strategies may include

Table 6.4

How Prepared Teachers Feel to Teach All Their Students to the State Standards, by Years of Experience (Percentage Distribution)

	0–4 Years	5–9 Years	10+ Years
Very well prepared	55	60	66
Only somewhat prepared	36	31	25
Not very well prepared	4	3	2
Does not apply/missing	5	6	7

pedagogy, of course. However, professional development also means weekly meetings to compare student work, to revise pacing calendars, to identify academic areas that need more attention, and to formulate schoolwide plans to address these weaknesses. It also means, we came to understand, developing a sense of teamwork and shared vision that motivates individual teachers to exert more effort than they would if they saw themselves only as individuals with their own immediate concerns.

We saw evidence of this type of professional development in the responses teachers gave to this question: Does your school have any strategies that have proven particularly effective in enhancing student achievement? In one rural high school, many teachers pointed to the three-hour block of time teachers had every Friday afternoon during which they could work with the principal on school planning. One teacher wrote,

> The collegial time we have is critical to our staff. Providing time for staff to work together on common problems provides a supportive group effort. We may not be able to solve all problems, but together we seem to solve a great many of them.

Many teachers in the school praised the principal for creating this atmosphere. One teacher wrote, "He supports our efforts and our new ideas of working with students."

Teachers in a suburban middle school echoed the importance of professional development in building a collegial and productive atmosphere. One teacher wrote,

> We meet together to work on assessments that meet the state standards. The key is that the teachers work together to reach the goals. We are given the time and materials necessary to achieve our goals, and we are supported in our quest. When the teachers are happy and feel like they are appreciated they pass this feeling on to the students who then feel more encouraged to achieve.

In other schools, however, this collegial atmosphere was a work in progress. In one suburban high school, the teachers seemed to believe the district leaders were commanding them to improve student achievement on the state's tests but were not including them in devising strategies for that improvement. One teacher wrote,

> How can we buy into any change when we are not included? I've been
> teaching for 24 years, and I love what I do, but administration at the district
> level has made me question how much longer I will stay with this profession.

Another at that school wrote that teachers have finally begun to meet in small groups to discuss the school's problems. However, a third wrote that the school's future success looked "bleak." After several years of lackluster performance, it still had not developed a plan to improve.

Class Size vs. Targeted Intervention

The emphasis that superintendents placed on professional development is entirely consistent with the general response to state standards we described in Chapter 3. A standards-based approach to education requires that teachers and administrators monitor what students are learning and identify deficiencies in that learning. It also requires that they act on those deficiencies. Accordingly, six superintendents identified their top priority for additional funds as interventions for struggling students. A superintendent at a large suburban district drew a direct link between the API and the allocation of resources.

> I would look at where our students are not performing compared to the API,
> and I'd want a direct link between those additional resources and what the
> weaknesses were.

The intervention mentioned most often by superintendents was small group tutoring in specific subject areas, usually in after-school programs.

In their budget workshops, principals also had the opportunity to allocate some of their budgets to targeted interventions. These interventions included after-school tutoring and summer school. They also included preschool, lengthening the school day, and lengthening the school year. This collection of programs saw the largest increase in expenditures as school budgets increased. With a 30 percent increase in their budgets, elementary school principals increased expenditures in this area by 159 percent, middle school principals by 140 percent, and high school principals by 112 percent. Much of this increase was focused on summer school and after-school tutoring.

In their open-ended responses to our survey, teachers often mentioned tutoring as an effective strategy in their schools. However, several pointed out that tutoring was effective only if students were motivated to seek additional help. One effective motivator was used by an elementary school in a rural area. Early in the school year, the school identified students who were at risk of being held back because they were falling behind in reading or mathematics. The school then notified their parents of this risk and offered them the services of the school's extensive after-school program, which combined tutoring with other less academic activities. Most parents gladly accepted the offer. In their open-ended responses, almost all teachers in this school cited this after-school program as an important ingredient in the school's academic success.

Not all superintendents saw targeted interventions as their highest priority, however. A few superintendents saw lowering class sizes for all as a way to help struggling students. A superintendent in an affluent suburban district told us

> The majority of our students are going to do fine no matter what happens, and that's kind of the nature of an affluent community. If you really want to reach the other students, our teachers see too many students. Our middle school teachers have a 200 student caseload. Out of that 200, 30 or 35 are not doing okay, but there's very little that a teacher can seriously do to help those students. Now if I could reduce the number of students that teacher sees by 20%, we've gained a lot of resources to help those kids.

The issue of reducing class sizes for all versus targeting struggling students is the basic school resource issue in the model we have sketched out in Chapter 3. The lower the class size for all students, the fewer students who fall behind, and thus the less need for intervention. However, it may well be more effective to let class sizes drift upward and redirect the resources gained from that increase to target support for the greater number of students who fall behind. Which strategy is more effective hinges on how class size in the regular program affects the percentage of students who fall behind and how effective targeted interventions are for those students. We are not aware of any direct research on this tradeoff. In any event, four superintendents responded that they would apply at least some funds to reducing class sizes in their regular program.

Conclusion

A school can employ resources in many different ways. The question "What do schools need?" is not well posed without the resource prices and the budget constraints that define realistic options. In the case of principals, we were able to pose this question precisely. For teachers and superintendents, however, it is more elusive.

Nevertheless, we learned something interesting from their responses. California schools are understaffed relative to schools in other states, and the teachers we interviewed identified specific areas in which staffing was inadequate. However, most superintendents did not emphasize staffing when asked what they would do with additional funds. Their biggest concern was the lack of time for professional development, or for teachers and administrators to examine test results and devise strategies for improving student learning.

By their answers, superintendents also identified an important issue in the way schools allocate their resources among students. Some superintendents favored decreasing class sizes for all students to allow teachers to focus more attention on struggling students. Others preferred to focus resources directly on those students through after-school tutoring or other targeted interventions. Opinions on this issue may also reflect the characteristics of students. If student backgrounds and preparations are diverse, targeted intervention may make more sense. If students are more homogeneous, however, lower class sizes may be the most effective strategy.

7. Implications for School Finance

The starting point for this report was the standards-based reform of California public schools. From our interviews with principals and superintendents and our survey of teachers, we conclude that this reform has fundamentally changed the way public schools envision their mission. Although implementation of this reform has been shaky at times, the underlying principles seem likely to endure. As a consequence, the state should rethink its other public school policies from the perspective of this new reform. In the case of public school finance, this imperative leads directly to the issue of resource adequacy: What resources do California schools need to accomplish the task the state has set out for them?

It should be no surprise that the standards reform would lead back to school finance. To a large extent, the reform was driven by the twin observations that the United States has spent vast sums on its public schools and yet the graduates of those schools do not appear to have learned very much, at least compared to students in other advanced countries. The conclusion many reached from these observations is that public schools are wasting scarce resources, leading to the notion that states need to spell out expectations more clearly and hold schools accountable for meeting those expectations. From that perspective, the abundance of resources is not really the issue. The issue is the wise use of those resources.

Yet, once the task for schools has been clearly defined, it is only natural to ask how much it will cost to achieve the task. If public schools are really wasting money, as some claim, should the state be providing them less? And, if so, how much less? Alternatively, if the state has asked schools to take on a challenging new task without providing them the accompanying resources, as others claim, what else do schools need?

In short, regardless of one's views about the efficiency of California's public schools, it is essential to ask how much money schools need to do the job the state has asked them to do. A clear set of standards leads directly to this question.

Our investigation of that question first led us to compare California schools with schools in other states. As we argued in *High Expectations, Modest Means,* California has relatively high expectations for its schools yet provides them relatively modest resources. This observation led us to ask a group of principals what resources they thought California schools need to meet the state's expectations. As we emphasized in our second report, *School Budgets and Student Achievement,* those principals agreed that more resources were necessary but differed greatly in their assessments of what schools need and what they would be able to achieve with different budget levels. These wide differences led to perhaps our most important conclusion: Although the adequacy question should be addressed, it is unlikely to have a definitive answer. Scientific evidence and expert opinion can get us only so far. The answer must inevitably involve the values and judgments of elected officials.

Standards-based reform brings another difficult issue to the forefront. For many years, researchers and policymakers have known that student achievement is related to the income of a student's family. Relative to other students, students from low-income families perform poorly on standardized achievement tests and are less likely to graduate from high school. This achievement gap may be partly due to the schools students attend. However, we doubt that this is the most important factor. As our teacher survey indicates, poor achievement of students from low-income families is also due to factors for which schools are not directly responsible.

These external factors pose a dilemma for school accountability measures. On one hand, it is not fair to hold schools accountable for factors outside their control. On the other hand, it is not democratic to have lower expectations for some children than for others. Low expectations can also become a self-fulfilling prophecy. With its school accountability system, California has attempted a compromise between these competing principles. It has set a high goal for every school, but it judges schools by their progress toward that goal. A superintendent of a large urban district quoted in Chapter 4 told us that it was advancement toward the target, rather than the target itself, that caused him and others in similar situations to "breathe a sigh of relief." As we pointed out, however, this relief is only temporary. If an 800 API is unrealistic for schools serving many low-income students, uniform progress toward that goal is also unrealistic. At some point, that growth will slow, making evident the underlying gap in achievement. By setting the same, high goal for every school, the state will ultimately focus attention on the achievement gap among schools with different student populations.

That gap leads naturally to the question of what additional resources schools in poor neighborhoods need to achieve state standards. As we noted in our first report, because of various state and federal categorical programs, the revenue school districts receive tends to increase with the percentage of their students who come from low-income families. As Chapter 5 demonstrated, those categorical programs do translate into additional resources at the school level. For the schools we visited, however, these additional categorical funds were partially offset by deficiencies in unrestricted revenues. In any event, regardless of the current distribution of revenue and resources among schools, the uniformity of expectations for all schools and the lower propensity of low-income schools to meet those expectations seem to indicate that additional investments should be focused on low-income schools and not spread widely across all schools.

Allocating Additional Funds to Low-Income Schools

A state focus on increasing resources in low-income schools must confront the reality that the state has little direct authority over school resources. The state allocates funds to school districts, not to schools. In that sense, school districts stand between the state and the objects of its concern. In allocating additional funds to school districts, how does the state ensure that those funds increase resources at low-income schools? One approach is typified by state categorical programs, such as Economic Impact Aid, that designate additional funds to schools serving low-income families. The federal Title I program performs a similar function. These programs impose many regulations on how funds are spent, which ensures that funds reach the intended target but also create bureaucratic obstacles for districts.

An alternative approach is to allocate more unrestricted funds to districts with many low-income pupils. For example, unrestricted funds could be allocated by a weighted-student formula, with students from low-income families having a higher weight than other students. Districts would then be free to allocate funds as they saw fit. Because of the state's accountability system, districts would have an incentive to allocate more funds to low-income schools, accomplishing the same objective as categorical programs without imposing bureaucratic obstacles. The state would be concerned with outcomes, not inputs. Districts would have the authority to allocate their funds to achieve those outcomes.

If California does decide to focus more resources on students from low-income families, it can choose between these two different approaches. A relevant factor in making that choice is how these approaches are perceived by district leaders. Accordingly, we asked the superintendents we visited a broad question about how they would like to see state funds allocated to districts. We gave them three general options: the current system, a modification of the current system with the same share of funds in categorical programs but fewer and broader categorical programs, and completely unrestricted funds.

The answers surprised us. Despite the increased flexibility it would give them, only three superintendents selected the third option of completely unrestricted funds. The remainder preferred a smaller number of broader categorical programs to the current system. From a superintendent's perspective, the choice between the first and second options seems straightforward. Broader categorical programs give them more flexibility. A superintendent of a high-performing suburban district described his rationale this way:

> I can understand the mentality that drives categoricals, but when it gets down to categoricals that say this money must be spent on textbooks versus this money must be spent on technology, that's when we really part ways because every district is so different. Every kid needs a textbook. Absolutely! But, because some districts didn't do a good job of managing that, the state has to come in with big block grants for textbooks when our kids already had textbooks. We'd like more flexibility.

Given the strong preference for reducing the number of categorical funding programs and broadening their scope, it would seem likely the superintendents would prefer to take the next step of completely unrestricted funds. Most superintendents chose not to take that step for two main reasons. The first concerned the allocation of funds to disadvantaged students. Some superintendents expressed a concern that if funds were completely unrestricted, local political pressures would make it difficult for districts to allocate more resources to schools with high concentrations of struggling students. A superintendent in a Central Valley city described this motivation aptly:

> Categoricals do keep some focus on poor kids and underperforming kids. In some districts, if superintendents were pressured by the more affluent and the powerful in the community, they might focus a lot of their attention on things that make for beautiful scenery or whatever without focusing on educational needs of some kids.

He would certainly favor the consolidation of some categorical programs such as instructional materials and technology but not programs such as federal Title I or state Economic Impact Aid, which focus funds on disadvantaged students.

A more common rationale for maintaining some categorical programs is that such programs are helpful in getting funds off the table during collective bargaining with teachers' and classified employee unions. Ideally, superintendents would prefer unrestricted funds, but they fear that completely unrestricted funds would go entirely to increases in salaries of unionized employees, leaving none for increasing school resources. One superintendent summed it up succinctly when he said, "I'd like a block grant that the union can't get their hands on."

The four superintendents who opted for completely unrestricted funds all discussed the implications of unrestricted funds for collective bargaining. A superintendent in Southern California preferred to have more flexibility because he believed his salaries were not competitive and he wanted to put more money on the bargaining table for his teachers. Two other superintendents acknowledged the power of the teachers' union in collective bargaining but were willing to fight those battles locally because they believed that categorical programs had led to large inefficiencies in the way funds are used. One of those superintendents was particularly concerned with the administrative burden of categorical programs:

> As someone who has served in five different states, it seems like you have to do an awful lot to earn back the money that you're supposed to receive. I have more management people in the budget and accounting piece of my organization than I do on the instructional piece. And, number two, the paperwork that's then transferred to principals, and to someone out there that they then have to go through. What do we really want principals to do? I truly believe they ought to be instructional leaders.

It is worth noting that the superintendent who expressed the strongest support for unrestricted funds leads one of California's largest districts. His comments deserve special note, not only because of the district but because they address so directly the concerns expressed by other superintendents. He did not see the teachers' union as a monolith that could overpower any school district at the bargaining table.

> I have never seen in our district the CTA [California Teachers Association] that superintendents describe behind closed doors, the CTA monolith that moves around the state, and you're going to be next. Never seen that in my district. It's always local interests, local concerns, local discussions.

He also articulated the important idea that the justification for categorical programs recedes when a state establishes a good accountability program.

> I believe that there are a multitude of ways to get results when it comes to student achievement. In an era of accountability, where you're removing school principals who don't get results, you ought to give them as wide discretion as possible to spend new dollars.

Despite this superintendent's persuasive argument, we cannot ignore the views of the majority of superintendents. Most found themselves facing a real dilemma. They preferred unrestricted funds in principle but would elect some categorical programs in practice because those programs keep funds off the bargaining table. One superintendent proposed a way to resolve this dilemma:

> One of the major inefficiencies in school district budgeting and financing is you've got 1,000 districts negotiating salaries. It is a ridiculous waste of everybody's time because we've got about one or two percent discretionary [funds] to mess with. It makes the whole system deviate from its mission. The

obvious alternative is you do a statewide salary schedule, you adjust for regional
cost of living, and you let the state bargain with the union statewide.

In elaborating on his proposal, the superintendent observed that the state
already has an indirect form of statewide collective bargaining. As several
superintendents told us, the percentage by which the legislature increases
unrestricted funds is routinely considered by teachers' unions as the
salary increase they can expect to receive through bargaining. Explicit
statewide collective bargaining would determine this salary increase
directly, thus removing one rationale for categorical programs. In
opposition to the possible advantages of statewide collective bargaining
are myriad potential disadvantages, including the potential of a statewide
teachers' strike and the difficulties of standardizing salary schedules and
working conditions across nearly 1,000 school districts.

Assigning Teachers to Schools

Collective bargaining at the district level is not inconsistent with the
goal of allocating additional funds to low-income schools. However,
most districts have negotiated contracts with their teachers that limit the
district's authority to move teachers from one school to another. These
limitations can frustrate district attempts to improve failing schools. A
superintendent in a large suburban district expressed this frustration:

> We have some schools that are failing, and we have known for years that we
> need to change the culture. And the only way we're going to change the
> culture is by a massive infusion of different people. One or two new teachers
> each year just get co-opted. I can't do what I want to do, which is to take eight
> teachers out at this place and replace them with eight teachers from another
> place.

Most teachers' contracts have provisions for involuntary transfers, but
the conditions are often vague and subject to grievance. A district is thus
reluctant to pursue such transfers. The superintendent of a large urban
district characterized the situation in his district:

> We debate with the union the whole issue of involuntary transfer, even within
> our contract. Our interpretation is that considerable authority rests with
> management. The association argues that the intent of the contract language is
> that all transfers are voluntary. So, let's say you've got a principal who taught
> at a blue ribbon school on this side of town and goes to another school
> downtown, with largely immigrants. She looks at her third grade staff and

decides that staff is not balanced with regard to age and maturity. So she reaches out to one of her veteran teachers at the blue ribbon school. Under the contract, there's already a couple thousand dollar bonus that will go with that, but the association would argue that the teacher has to be asked and then, if the teacher says yes, there ought to be incentives over and above what's already there.

Even in districts where the contract language clearly gives the district the right to transfer teachers, districts may be reluctant to "throw their weight around." One district in our sample was uniquely different in this regard. It had bargained the right to transfer teachers without their consent and then developed a whole series of remedial actions it could take with teachers who were not working out at a particular school. The ability to transfer teachers was an important condition the district held in reserve during this process, however. As the superintendent described it,

Our focus was to help all teachers to succeed, but at the end of it lies the ability to transfer. We've only force-transferred two teachers, although we have moved one hundred teachers in a year's time.

The superintendent was pleased to point out that, as a result of these numerous voluntary moves, the district had its most qualified teachers at its lowest-income schools.

A state focus on increasing funds for low-income schools could help other districts carry out the type of transfers this district was able to make. If schools serving low-income students have more funds than other schools in a district, teachers are more likely to find these schools to be attractive assignments. Bonuses for teachers in these schools could provide another incentive.

Conclusion

High standards for all public schools will inevitably focus attention on schools serving low-income students. These schools will find it harder to meet those expectations than other schools—a situation that provides further impetus for the necessity of increasing the resources of those schools. One approach to this goal is to build on existing categorical programs. Another approach is to allocate more unrestricted funds to the districts housing these schools.

A discussion of the advantages and disadvantages of these two approaches leads directly to the issue of school governance. By establishing an ambitious set of standards for all public schools, the state has claimed authority over what schools in California ought to do. Because of court cases and popular initiatives, it has also gained almost complete control of the finances of public schools. From the state's point of view, the most coherent policy is to set expectations for schools, to allocate funds to school districts, and to let districts determine how to use those funds to best to meet the state's expectations.

Because of the process by which districts are governed, however, this appealing policy may fail to accomplish the state's objectives. Local voters still elect school boards who hire and fire district administrators, determine the allocation of school budgets, and set other school policies. Districts also bargain with their employee unions over salaries, benefits, and working conditions. In addition to the state's expectations, a district's leaders must also be concerned about the interests of local voters and employee unions. These interests may not always coincide with the state's interests. If the state cedes complete authority over spending decisions to districts, it may find that districts do not put much weight on state interests. Accordingly, the state might reasonably retain some control over how district funds are spent. Categorical programs perform this function.

Local governance is an issue only if the interests of local voters differ from the interests of all voters in the state. The former elect school board representatives and thus determine school board policy. The latter elect the state legislature and other state officials who ultimately determine the state's expectations for its schools. If the interests of local voters are in perfect harmony with the interests of state voters, local governance of schools does not pose a problem for the state. The concern that local governance will thwart state intentions must therefore rest on the perception that there are differences between the interests of local and state voters. In the aggregate, of course, local voters are state voters. This should cause us to ask how much political support there is for the kind of school finance policy that follows logically from the state's high expectations for all schools. If school districts find it politically difficult to allocate more funds to schools serving low-income students, is it realistic for the state legislature to support such policies?

This question is particularly salient because, on average, schools in California have fewer resources than schools in other states. Parents in affluent California suburbs compare their schools with those in similar suburbs in other large states and quickly discover that their schools have larger classes, fewer counselors, and fewer resources overall. It seems difficult to believe that these parents will lend strong political support to investing additional public funds solely in schools in low-income neighborhoods when they perceive their own schools as inadequately funded. The logic of state standards may soon collide with the realities of pluralistic politics.

A recent PPIC poll asked a random sample of Californians to address this issue (Baldassare, 2005). In particular, respondents were asked, "Should school districts in lower-income areas get more resources from the state than other school districts?" Sixty-four percent of adults responded in the affirmative. Among those with household incomes exceeding $80,000 per year, this response was slightly less frequent, 58 percent. Nonetheless, regardless of their own income, a clear majority of respondents supported the concept of allocating more revenue to school districts in low-income areas. The question was vague, however, about the magnitude of those additional allocations. If substantial additional resources are necessary for schools in low-income areas to meet state expectations, will public opinion continue to be as positive?

Appendix A

Data Sources

This appendix describes the data sources used throughout the report.

Academic Performance Index, School Characteristic Index, Participation in Subsidized Lunch Program

Data about the API, the School Characteristic Index (SCI), and the percentage of students participating in the free or reduced-price lunch program came from the API base year files maintained by the California Department of Education. The percentage of students participating in the free or reduced-price lunch program in these files refers to the percentage of students tested who are participants in the lunch program. Tables 2.2 and 2.3 use the 2003 base file. (One school was missing an API score for 2003, because not enough students at the school took one part of the test. For this school, we used its 2002 API score in the calculations.) Figure 4.1 uses the base files from 2001, 2002, and 2003.

School Description and Enrollment

The number of schools and enrollment data in Chapter 2 are from the California Basic Educational Data System (CBEDS) maintained by the California Department of Education. Enrollment is from the 2002–2003 school enrollment file called "enrsch02." Data on school and district type are from the March 2005 file "List of California Public School Districts and Schools." We include junior high schools in our middle school category.

Census Characteristics of Sample Schools

The census characteristics come from the 2000 U.S. Census, summary file 3. We used census maps to determine which tracts were in the school attendance zones. We aggregated the tract-level data to the school attendance zone area, weighting the tract characteristics by the share of the tract's geographic area in the school attendance zone.

Teacher Survey Data

One school was omitted from Table 5.10 because it had completed an earlier version of the teacher survey in which the age categories for textbooks were somewhat different.

Appendix B

Sampling Method

To select the schools for our site visits, we designed a stratified random sampling procedure that ensured several goals. We wanted to include schools from all regions of the state. We required roughly equal numbers of elementary, middle, and high schools from a combination of unified, elementary, and high school districts. We also sought schools that served many low-income students and others that served a more affluent student body. In considering the low-income schools, we wanted to ensure that a large portion of those schools were doing well academically relative to schools serving similar students.

To satisfy the dual goals of minimizing the number of school districts while ensuring equal numbers of elementary, middle, and high schools, we selected a trio of schools (where a trio consists of one elementary, one middle, and one high school) from either one unified school district or a combination of an elementary and high school district. We first determined the number of trios to select from each region of the state. Table B.1 shows this breakdown. For example, we selected three trios (i.e., three elementary, three middle, and three high schools) from Northern California. We selected two trios from unified districts and one trio from a combination of an elementary and a high school district. In total, we selected 30 trios (i.e., 90 schools) from 24 unified schools districts, six elementary school districts, and six high school districts. To ensure that our sample represented all areas of the state, we oversampled from relatively smaller regions and undersampled from the Los Angeles area.

Next, we classified each school into one of three categories based on the SES of its students and its API score. The three categories are low-SES with a relatively low API, low-SES with a relatively high API, and high-SES. Within the high-SES category, we did not distinguish between low-API and high-API schools. Although the main body of the report defines SES solely as a function of the percentage of students in

Table B.1

Stratified Random Sample

Region	No. of Trios Selected	From Unified Districts	From District Pairs (Elem. + High)	Low-SES High-API	Low-SES Low-API	High-SES	As % of Selected Sample
Northern California	3	2	1	1	1	1	10
Bay Area	6	5	1	2	2	2	20
Central Coast	3	2	1	1	1	1	10
Central Valley	6	5	1	2	2	2	20
Los Angeles region	7	6	1	3	2	2	23
San Diego/Imperial	5	4	1	2	1	2	17
Total trios	30	24	6	11	9	10	
Total schools	90	72	18	33	27	30	
As % of selected sample	100	80	20	37	30	33	

the free or reduced-price lunch program, for sampling purposes we define SES using the School Characteristic Index (SCI). The SCI is a composite of student background characteristics. Schools with a high SCI have relatively low rates of student poverty. They also enroll students with relatively more educated parents.

Our definition of high-SES schools are those with a three-year average SCI in the top two-thirds of the SCI distribution for its school level (elementary, middle, or high). Although two-thirds of the schools fall in this category, we drew only one-third of our sample from this category. Conversely, we drew two-thirds of our sample from low-SES schools, although they constitute only one-third of California schools. We oversampled low-SES schools, because those schools are furthest away from the state's API goal, and we wanted to better understand the challenges they faced in trying to close the gap.

Within the low-SES school category, we divided schools into high-API and low-API schools based on their Similar Schools Ranking during the three years before our study. Schools with an average ranking in the top 20 percent were considered high-API schools; those in the bottom 80 percent were considered low-API schools. We oversampled from these high-API schools so we could learn what the relatively successful schools were doing to meet the challenges presented by the state's accountability system.

Table B.1 shows the number of school trios from each SES-API category that we selected from each region. For example, from Northern California, we selected one trio of schools from each of the three SES-API categories. In other words, we selected one elementary school from each category, one middle school from each category, and one high school from each category. In San Diego, however, we selected two trios of low-SES, high-API schools but only one trio of low-SES, low-API schools.

To carry out this procedure, we first randomly selected the prespecified number of school districts from each region, weighting by the enrollment in each district. If these districts contained the appropriate mix of schools based on the number we required from each SES-API category, those districts became part of our sample. Within those districts, we then randomly selected the prespecified number of schools from each SES-API category. Because we wanted our ultimate sample of schools to reflect schools serving many of the state's students, the random sampling procedure weighted schools by enrollment and excluded small schools with fewer than 200 students. We did not require all schools in the high-SES trio to come from just one district. For example, the high-SES elementary school could come from district A whereas the high-SES middle school could come from district B and the high-SES high school from district C. If the universe of schools within the selected districts did not include the appropriate number of schools we required from each SES-API category, we randomly selected another set of districts. We resampled districts until the schools they contained met our SES-API category requirements. Ultimately, this procedure ensured that we visited a variety of schools throughout the state while simultaneously ensuring a random mechanism of selection.

Appendix C

School Finance Data

Until recently, California lacked the ability to compare education resources at the school site level. The implementation of the new Standardized Account Code Structure (SACS) by all of the state's school districts represents a major step toward removing this stumbling block. As of 2003–2004, all California school districts report their financial data to the state using SACS. As the name implies, SACS requires that all districts categorize each transaction using a standardized code. Essentially, this code describes the source of the funds, what the funds were used to purchase, and the purpose of the expenditure. Although the data are reported to the state at the district level, the code also allows districts to track expenditures to the school level. In contrast to the accounting procedures previously used by school districts, the SACS structure provides a much richer and more consistent description of each financial transaction.

We developed a method of categorizing expenditures using the SACS classification to produce comparable, consistent measures of spending across individual school sites located in different school districts. We designed a questionnaire to gather specific expenditure data for the 2001–2002 school year from district business offices. Of the original 49 schools, we were able to obtain school-level data for about 41 schools in 19 districts. Fifteen of the districts had converted to SACS by 2001. For the remaining four districts, we tried to ensure that they reported financial information in a manner consistent with the definitions used in our SACS-based questionnaire.

As Chapter 5 demonstrated, we used these data to compare expenditures between high- and low-SES schools. That task only scratches the surface of what can be done with the SACS data. In this appendix, we provide a detailed description of the SACS data and our classification system. We also analyze how the composition of school resources varies among elementary, middle, and high schools.

Standardized Account Code Structure

In SACS, each transaction is given a code composed of seven fields and 22 digits. The fields identify the fund, object, resource, function, project year, goal, and school site.[1] The main fields we used to identify resources were the school site, fund, resource, object, and function.

The school site field identifies the school for which the expenditure was made. Currently, school districts are not required to use this field, yet all but one district we gathered SACS data from had used it. We assumed that the methods of allocating costs to the site level were reasonably consistent among the districts in our sample. The one elementary district not using the school field had a small number of similar-sized schools. The district's business officer indicated that all of these schools received similar amounts of per-pupil funding, from the same sources. Accordingly, for this district, we allocated district-level expenditures to the sample school based on the share of districtwide enrollment that its students represented. If the school site field were to become mandatory, it would be necessary to develop standards for allocating revenues and expenditures to the school site level—something that the California Department of Education has not yet done.

The fund refers to a self-balancing set of accounts that may be used for general expenditures (as in the case of the General Fund) or that are segregated and limited to special purposes (e.g., Cafeteria Fund, Building Fund).

The resource field refers to the source of the funds. For example, revenue limits, special education, and Economic Impact Aid are all identified as separate resources. Therefore, this field allows activities funded from unrestricted sources (codes 0000 to 1999) to be separated from those funded from restricted, or categorical, sources (codes 2000 to 9999). It also enables school districts to track activities that have reporting requirements or restrictions on their use, such as lottery funds (1100) or the federal Title I program (3000 to 3299).

The object and function codes describe the purpose of the expenditure. The object code refers to the specific services or

---

[1]Additional information on SACS is provided in California Department of Education (2001).

84

commodities that are purchased, such as salaries, fringe benefits, textbooks, utilities, equipment, and the like. The function field designates a transaction's general operational area, type of activity, or both. Examples of function codes include general and special education instruction, school board and superintendent activities, and plant maintenance. For example, spending on salaries (an object) can be broken down by whether it is for general instruction classes or special education classes. Administrator salaries (an object) can be broken down into school administration or district administration using the functions.

The project year field is used to identify funding sources—such as federal grants—in which the funding period spans more than one state fiscal year.[2] The goal field is used to track a transaction's objective related to an instructional setting or a special population. Examples of goals include K–12 regular education, bilingual education, and alternative schools. We did not use the goal field to categorize expenditure data.

Our Questionnaire

To ensure comparability of data across districts and school sites, we gathered data from school business offices in specific combinations of the codes for fund, resource, function, object, and site. We defined these combinations to include every piece of expenditure data we needed, without omissions or double-counting.

Our data gathering efforts focused on the core functions of K–12 education. For purposes of our study, we defined these core resources as operational expenditures from a school district's General Fund or Deferred Maintenance Fund. We excluded expenditures in areas that are not core functions, such as expenditures associated with enterprise (fee-for-service) activities, child nutrition (food services), child care and

---

[2]For example, suppose that a school district received a grant for the federal fiscal year running from October 1, 2002, through September 30, 2003, and another grant for October 1, 2003, through September 30, 2004. The grant activities during the state fiscal year 2003–2004 (which runs from July 1 through June 30) would include three months of expenditures in the federal project year 2002–2003 (coded as 03) and nine months of activities in federal project year 2003–2004 (coded as 04). For fund sources in which the funding period coincides with the state fiscal year, the project year field is not used.

development, and adult education. In addition, we did not include any capital expenditures for construction, reconstruction, or modernization of school facilities.

Our questionnaire classified expenditures into three broad areas: direct school site, indirect school site, and district-level expenditure attributable to the school. Direct school site expenditures include general education, special education, and other federal, state, and local expenditures that are identified with the specific school site. Examples include the salary and benefits of teachers, administrators, or support staff who work full-time at the specified school site.

Indirect school site expenditures also include general education, special education, and other federal, state, and local expenditures. In contrast to direct school site expenditures, however, indirect school site expenditures are not directly charged to specific school sites. An example would be when a school district uses funds for instructional materials to purchase textbooks centrally and then distributes these books to its schools, rather than allocating these funds to individual schools.

District-level expenditures include the operations of the district's administrative offices (e.g., superintendent's office, board of education, budget office, personnel office), supervision of instruction charged to the district's central administrative office (e.g., instructional research, curriculum development), and pupil services charged to the central administrative office (e.g., psychological or academic testing services provided districtwide). We also defined district-level expenditures to include pupil transportation; centralized maintenance, operations, grounds, and custodial functions that benefit school sites; insurance; utilities; and communications.

To obtain a comprehensive picture of the resources available to support each school site's operations, expenditures in the indirect school site and district-level categories were allocated to each school site using various pro-ration formulas. For example, indirect school site expenditures on K–8 instructional materials were allocated to an individual school site based on the proportion of districtwide K–8 enrollment that its K–8 students represented. Similarly, indirect school site expenditures on the School Improvement Program in grades K–6 were allocated to an individual school site based on the proportion of districtwide K–6 enrollment that its K–6 students represented. District-level expenditures, in contrast, were allocated to individual school sites based on the proportion of districtwide enrollment represented by the school site's enrollment. One district we visited did not keep track separately of costs incurred by the central district office (i.e., district administration, instructional supervision, and pupil services). Rather, it spread these costs across school sites without specifying how much was allocated to each. Had we known the central district office costs, we would have allocated them to the school sites based on enrollment. Because we could not determine these costs, we made no changes to the school site data—thereby accepting the district's method for distributing costs to its school sites. With the exception of this district, the prorated indirect and district expenditures are effectively the same for all schools within a district, therefore we omit these expenditures from the tables in Chapter 5.

Within each of these three broad areas, we used a combination of resource, function, and object codes to classify expenditures. Tables C.1 through C.3 show this system for direct school site, indirect school site, and district-level expenditures, respectively. The numbers in each cell refer to transaction codes used in SACS.

Within the direct school site and indirect school site areas, we primarily used the SACS resource codes to distinguish among types of expenditures. The following presents an example of how the tables are interpreted. To identify direct school site expenditures on federal restricted programs other than special education, go to the row labeled "Other restricted: federal." The first column, labeled "Resource," indicates that this category includes resource codes 3000 through 3299, 3500 through 4999, and 5500 through 5999. These ranges describe all federal resources (which range from 3000 to 5999) except special education (3300 through 3499) and federal child development and child nutrition programs (5000 to 5499). The next column describes the function codes used to capture these federal programs. The codes noted (1000 to 5999 and 7000 to 7999) include all functions except enterprise activities (6000 to 6999), plant services (8000 to 8999), and other outgo (9000 to 9999). The third column, "Object," indicates that this

Table C.1

Classification of Direct School Site Expenditures

Expenditure type	Resource	Function	Object	Site
General education (unrestricted)	0000–1999	1000–5999 7000–7999	Any except 5400, 5500, 5900	Specific school site
Special education	3300–3499 6500–6530	1000–5999 7000–7999	Any except 5400, 5500, 5900	Specific school site
Other restricted				
Federal	3000–3299 3500–4999 5500–5999	1000–5999 7000–7999	Any except 5400, 5500, 5900	Specific school site
State (excluding pupil transportation)	6210–6499 6540–7018 7035–7149 7250–7999	1000–5999 7000–7999	Any except 5400, 5500, 5900	Specific school site
Local	8000–9999	1000–5999 7000–7999	Any except 5400, 5500, 5900	Specific school site
Maintenance/operations/ grounds/custodial	Any	8000–8499	Any except 5400, 5500, 5900	Specific school site

NOTES: Numbers refer to transaction codes used in California's SACS. All expenditures are from the general fund (fund 01) except maintenance/operations/ grounds/custodial, which also includes expenditures from the deferred maintenance fund (fund 14). All expenditures for enterprise activities (functions 6000–6999) are excluded.

category of other federal restricted programs includes expenditures for all objects other than 5400 (insurance), 5500 (utilities), and 5900 (communications). Finally, the fourth column indicates that we want to collect this information for the specific school site or sites (as indicated by the appropriate three-digit site code) that are included in our sample. School site expenditures on maintenance, operations, grounds, and

Table C.2

Classification of Indirect School Site Expenditures

Expenditure type	Resource	Function	Object	Site
General education (unrestricted)	0000–1999	1000–5999 7000–7999	Any except 5400, 5500, 5900	All except school sites
Special education	3300–3499 6500–6530	1000–5999 7000–7999	Any except 5400, 5500, 5900	All except school sites
Other restricted				
Federal	3000–3299 3500–4999 5500–5999	1000–5999 7000–7999	Any except 5400, 5500, 5900	All except school sites
State (excluding pupil transportation)	6210–6499 6540–7018 7035–7149 7250–7999	1000–5999 7000–7999	Any except 5400, 5500, 5900	All except school sites
Local	8000–9999	1000–5999 7000–7999	Any except 5400, 5500, 5900	All except school sites
Maintenance/operations/ grounds/custodial	Any	8000–8499	Any except 5400, 5500, 5900	All except school sites

NOTES: Numbers refer to transaction codes used in California's SACS. All expenditures are from the general fund (fund 01) except maintenance/operations/ grounds/custodial, which also includes expenditures from the deferred maintenance fund (fund 14). All expenditures for enterprise activities (functions 6000–6999) are excluded.

custodial services were defined in terms of function (8000 to 8499). Expenditures were then further classified by object.

For the district-level expenditures, we primarily used the SACS function codes to classify administrative expenditures. Expenditures for pupil transportation were primarily defined in terms of resource codes (7230 to 7240). Expenditures for insurance, utilities, and communications were defined in terms of object codes (5400, 5500, and 5900, respectively). These three object codes were the ones excluded from all the other categories.

Table C.3

Classification of District-Level Direct School Site Expenditures

Expenditure type	Resource	Function	Object	Site
Administration				
District	Any except 3300–3499 6500–6530 7230–7240	7000–7999	Any except 5400, 5500, 5900	District office
Instructional supervision	Any except 3300–3499 6500–6530 7230–7240	2100–2149	Any except 5400, 5500, 5900	District office
Pupil services	Any except 3300–3499 6500–6530 7230–7240	3110–3179 3900–3999	Any except 5400, 5500, 5900	District office
Pupil transportation (excluding insurance)				
Regular	7230	1000–5999 7000–7999	Any except 5400, 5500, 5900	All except school sites
Special education	7240	1000–5999 7000–7999	Any except 5400, 5500, 5900	All except school sites
Bus replacement	7235	1000–5999 7000–7999	Any except 5400, 5500, 5900	All except school sites
Maintenance/operations/ grounds/custodial	Any	8000–8499	Any except 5400, 5500, 5900	Districtwide, maintenance yard
Facilities acquisition and construction	Any	8500	6100–6200	All
Insurance	Any	1000–5999 7000–8499	5400	All
Utilities	Any	8000–8499	5500	All school sites
Communications	Any	1000–5999 7000–8499	5900	All school sites

NOTES: Numbers refer to transaction codes used in California's SACS. All expenditures are from the general fund (fund 01) except maintenance/operations/grounds/custodial, which also includes expenditures from the deferred maintenance fund (fund 14). All expenditures for enterprise activities (functions 6000–6999) are excluded.

A Financial Picture of Our Schools

In Chapter 5, we identified expenditures primarily by their resource and function codes to describe spending from unrestricted and categorical sources. We can also classify expenditures by the specific goods or services that school districts purchase, i.e., the object code. Table C.4 shows the breakdown for elementary, middle, and high schools. We divide expenditures into seven areas. Teacher compensation represents the costs of teachers' salaries and benefits, including the district's contribution to the state teachers' retirement system (CalSTRS).[3] Other certificated employees are nonteaching employees, such as school administrators and counselors, who are nevertheless required to hold a state-issued certificate. Classified employees, also referred to as noncertificated employees, include such categories as instructional aides, clerical support personnel, and

Table C.4

Expenditures per Pupil, by School Type, 2001–2002

Expenditure Type	Elem. $ Amount	Elem. % of Total	Middle $ Amount	Middle % of Total	High $ Amount	High % of Total
Teacher compensation	3,487	50.4	3,204	46.2	3,506	47.8
Other certificated compensation	672	9.7	926	13.3	954	13.0
Classified compensation	1,654	23.9	1,719	24.8	1,843	25.1
Materials and supplies	418	6.0	468	6.7	405	5.5
Services and operating expenses	611	8.8	547	7.9	530	7.2
Equipment	58	0.8	61	0.9	91	1.2
Other	18	0.3	14	0.2	1	0.0
Total	6,918	100.0	6,939	100.0	7,328	100.0

[3]One district in our sample did not use SACS to track teachers' salaries to the school site level. In this case, we assigned to the schools in this district a cost for teacher salaries based on each school's share of the teachers in the district. A non-SACS district failed to separate employee benefits (e.g., retirement and health insurance) between certificated and classified staff. Rather, the district simply reported a grand total expenditure for all benefits. We divided up those total benefit expenditures into certificated and classified employee benefits based on the proportion of total salaries represented by certificated salaries versus classified salaries, respectively.

maintenance workers. Materials and supplies include textbooks, other books, and instructional supplies. Finally, services and operating expenses include utilities, contract services, and insurance.

Total per-pupil spending at elementary and middle schools in our sample was nearly identical. Average per-pupil spending for the 14 elementary schools in our sample was almost the same as that for the 13 middle schools in our sample—$6,918 and $6,939, respectively. Per-pupil spending on elementary schools in our sample ranged from $5,873 to $8,450; per-pupil spending for middle schools ranged from $5,668 to $8,554. Average per-pupil spending in the 14 high schools in our sample totaled $7,328—5.6 percent higher than that of our middle schools. Per-pupil spending in high schools in our sample ranged from $5,934 to $9,077.

The distribution of expenditures by object category was remarkably similar between middle and high schools. However, elementary schools spent a larger proportion of their total per-pupil funding on teacher compensation than did middle and high schools, most likely as a result of K–3 CSR. In contrast, elementary schools spent a smaller share than middle and high schools on compensation for nonteacher certificated personnel. This difference reflects the greater number of vice principals and counselors per pupil that middle and high schools have, compared to elementary schools.

The only expenditure categories in which per-pupil spending at our high schools was substantially less than that in the elementary or middle schools were services and operating expenses and materials and supplies. To the extent that services and operating expenses have a large fixed cost component, the differences in per-pupil spending for this purpose may simply reflect economies of scale. For materials and supplies, however, it is not clear why per-pupil expenditures at the middle schools should be higher than those at the elementary and high schools. This puzzling result may simply be the product of our small sample size.

References

Baldassare, Mark, *Special Survey on Education,* Public Policy Institute of California, San Francisco, California, April 2005.

California Department of Education, *California School Accounting Manual,* 2001 ed., Sacramento, California, 2001.

The Education Trust-West, *California's Hidden Teacher Spending Gap: How State and District Budgeting Practices Shortchange Poor and Minority Students and Their Schools,* Oakland, California, 2005.

Finn, Chester E., and Michael J. Petrilli (eds.), *The State of State Standards: 2000,* Thomas B. Fordham Foundation, Washington, D.C., 2000

Rivkin, Steven G., Eric A. Hanushek, and John F. Kain, "Teachers, Schools, and Academic Achievement," *Econometrica,* Vol, 73, No. 2, March 2005, pp. 417–458.

Rogosa, David, *Interpretive Notes for the Academic Performance Index,* Stanford University, Stanford, California, November 20, 2000.

Rose, Heather, Jon Sonstelie, Ray Reinhard, and Sharmaine Heng, *High Expectations, Modest Means: The Challenge Facing California's Public Schools,* Public Policy Institute of California, San Francisco, California, 2003.

Rose, Heather, Jon Sonstelie, and Peter Richardson, *School Budgets and Student Achievement in California: The Principal's Perspective,* Public Policy Institute of California, San Francisco, California, 2004.

Roza, Marguerite, and Paul T. Hill, "How Within-District Spending Inequities Help Some Schools to Fail," in Diane Ravitch, ed., *Brookings Papers on Education Policy 2004,* Brookings Institution, Washington, D.C., 2004.

About the Authors

HEATHER ROSE

Heather Rose is a research fellow at the Public Policy Institute of California, specializing in the economics of education. She has published work on school finance, college affirmative action policies, and the relationship between high school curriculum, test scores, and subsequent earnings. Her current research projects focus on school board politics and teacher salaries. She holds a B.A. in economics from the University of California, Berkeley, and an M.A. and Ph.D. in economics from the University of California, San Diego.

JON SONSTELIE

Jon Sonstelie is a professor of economics at the University of California, Santa Barbara. His research interests include several areas in public finance and urban economics, including the effect of public school quality on private school enrollment, the incidence of the property tax, the demand for public school spending, the economics of rationing by waiting, and the effect of transportation innovations on residential locations. He was previously a research fellow at Resources for the Future. He holds a B.A. from Washington State University and a Ph.D. in economics from Northwestern University.

RAY REINHARD

Ray Reinhard is assistant secretary for education policy in the administration of Governor Arnold Schwarzenegger. Before taking his current position, he was an education specialist at the Public Policy Institute of California. Before joining the institute in 2002, he was a school district chief business officer. Between 1979 and 1999, he held various administrative, supervisory, and research positions in Sacramento with the California Department of Education, the Governor's Office, and the Legislative Analyst's Office. He holds an M.P.P. in public policy from the University of California, Berkeley, and an A.B. in economics and urban studies from Dartmouth College.

Related PPIC Publications

High Expectations, Modest Means: The Challenge Facing California's Public Schools
Heather Rose, Jon Sonstelie, Ray Reinhard, and Sharmaine Heng

School Budgets and Student Achievement in California: The Principal's Perspective
Heather Rose, Jon Sonstelie, and Peter Richardson

School Finance and California's Master Plan for Education
Jon Sonstelie and Peter Richardson (editors)

Equal Resources, Equal Outcomes? The Distribution of School Resources and Student Achievement in California
Julian R. Betts, Kim S. Rueben, and Anne Danenberg

Class Size Reduction, Teacher Quality, and Academic Achievement in California Public Elementary Schools
Christopher Jepsen and Steven Rivkin

For Better or For Worse? School Finance Reform in California
Jon Sonstelie, Eric Brunner, and Kenneth Ardon